Imagine Art

Works of Art
by
Dr. Ruth Velikovsky Sharon
and
Elisheva Velikovsky

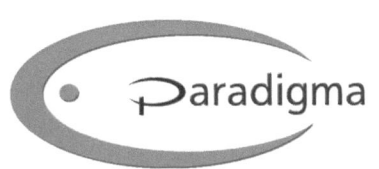

Copyright © 2009 by   Ruth Velikovsky Sharon, Ph.D.

                                Internet: www.ruthvelikovskysharon.com
                                e-mail: ruthvsharonphd@verizon.net

All rights reserved. No part of this book may be reproduced or transmitted in any form or by any means, electronic or mechanical, including photocopying, recording, or by any information storage and retrieval system, without permission in writing from the copyright owner, except by reviewers who may quote brief passages to be printed in a magazine or newspaper.

Photographs: Mark Czajkowski

Published by   Paradigma Ltd.
                                Internet: www.paradigma-publishing.com
                                e-mail: info@paradigma-publishing.com

ISBN 978-1-906833-02-2

Contents

Introduction
p. 5

Elisheva Velikovsky
p. 7

Ruth Velikovsky Sharon, PhD.
p. 23

Introduction

The name of Velikovsky is mainly known from the scientific and historical discoveries of Dr. Immanuel Velikovsky and the related "Velikovsky affair", which has been compared in extension and importance to the "Galileo affair" four centuries ago.

Far less known is the artistic dimension in the Velikovsky family, mainly expressed by

Elisheva (or "Elis") Velikovsky
and
Ruth Velikovsky Sharon, PhD.,

the wife and daughter of Immanuel Velikovsky.

For everyone interested in and fond of visual and plastic arts this booklet will give an exhaustive overview of the remarkable range of the works of these two artists.

If there is interest or inquiry about any of the works, please contact:

> Dr. Ruth Velikovsky Sharon
> 50 Deer Path
> Princeton, New Jersey 08540
> USA
> email: ruthvsharonphd@verizon.net
> telephone: 1-609-921-0959
> cell: 609-731-0261

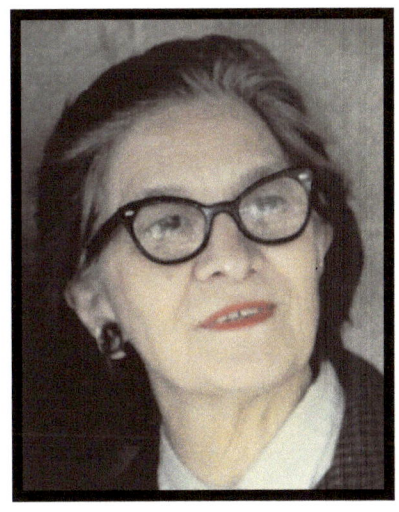

Elisheva Velikovsky

Elis (Elisheva) Velikovsky was born in Hamburg, Germany in 1895. Her maiden name was Kramer.
She studied violin with Adolph Busch in Berlin, Germany from 1920 to 1923. After marrying Dr. Immanuel Velikovsky, they moved to Palestine where she became the leader of the Palestine String Quartet from 1928 to 1938.
She took trips to the Grand Chaumier in Paris, where she studied drawing.
In 1939, upon moving to New York, she studied sculpture at Columbia University from 1940 till 1945 under Oronzo Maldarelli.

Her sculptures were included in annual shows at exhibitions of sculpture:

The New York Historical Society 1943
Whitney Museum 1946, 1947, 1955
Pennsylvania Academy of Fine Art 1952
Audubon Annual Exhibit 1946, 1952
Montclair Art Museum 1955, 1958

She repeatedly exhibited (by invitation) at the Whitney Museum and the Pennsylvania Academy of Fine Arts and was included in the Metropolitan Museum of Art (New York 1950). This was a National Competitors Sculpture Exhibition of over 5000 works submitted and 94 were accepted. Her sculpture "Caryatid" was the first of the 50 photographs in the catalogue of the Museum.

One man show at Columbia University, New York 1945

One man show at Princeton University, Princeton, New Jersey 1964

She received the first prize in Sculpture from the New Jersey State exhibition at the Montclair Museum, New Jersey 1958.

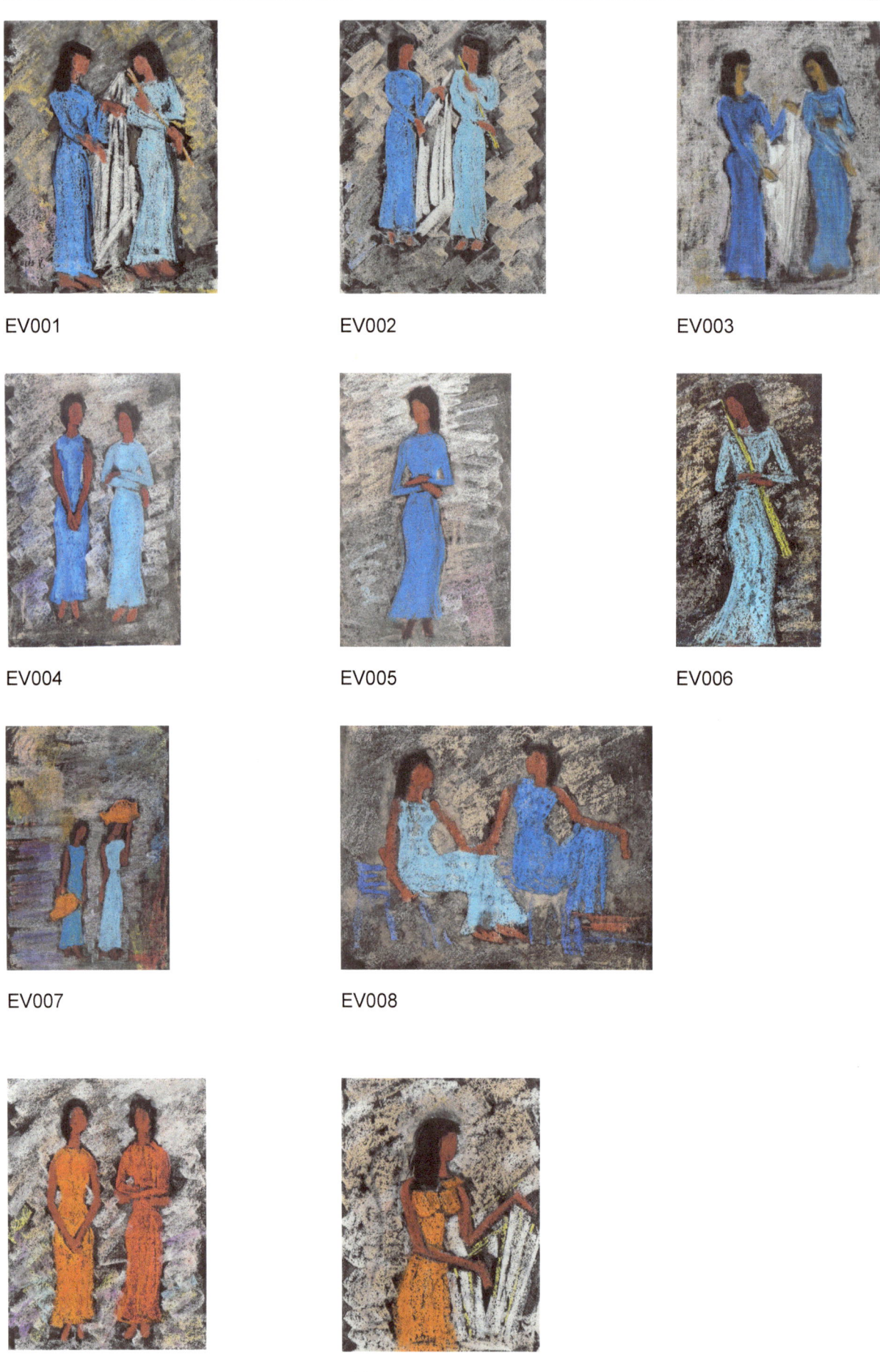

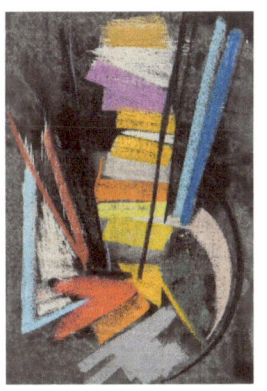

EV011

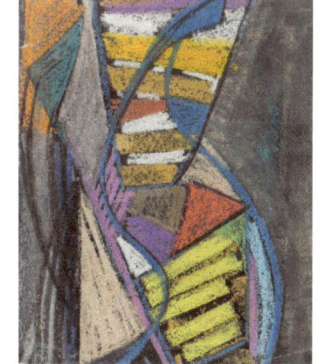

EV012

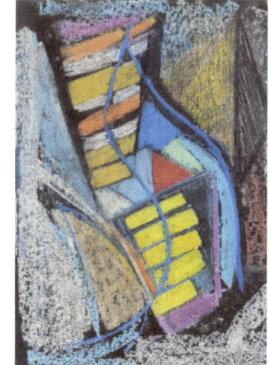

EV013

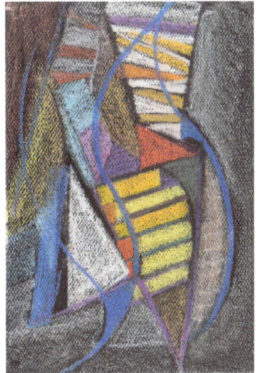

EV014

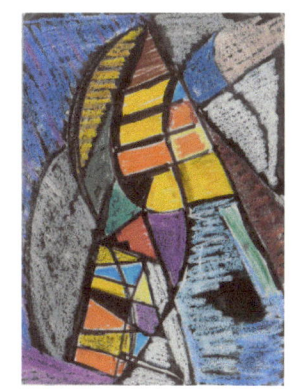

EV015

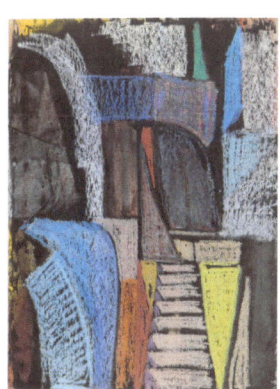

EV016

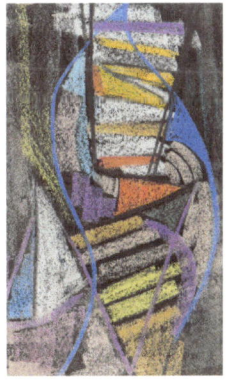

EV017

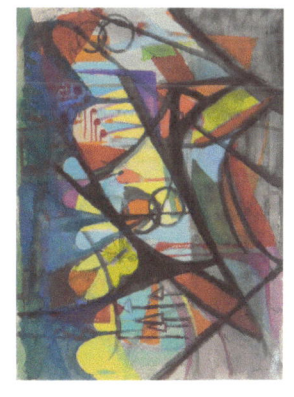

EV018

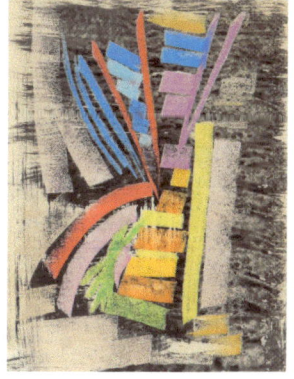

EV019

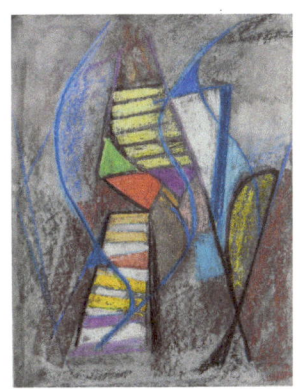

EV020

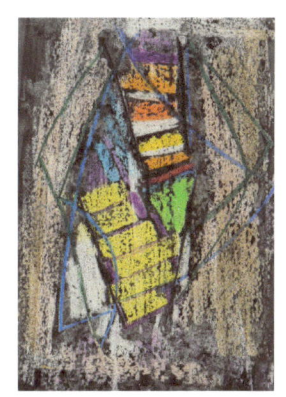

EV021

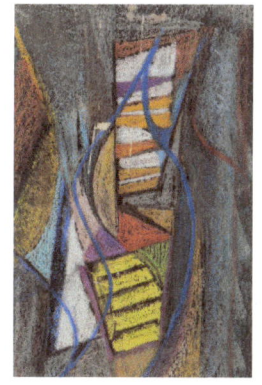

EV022

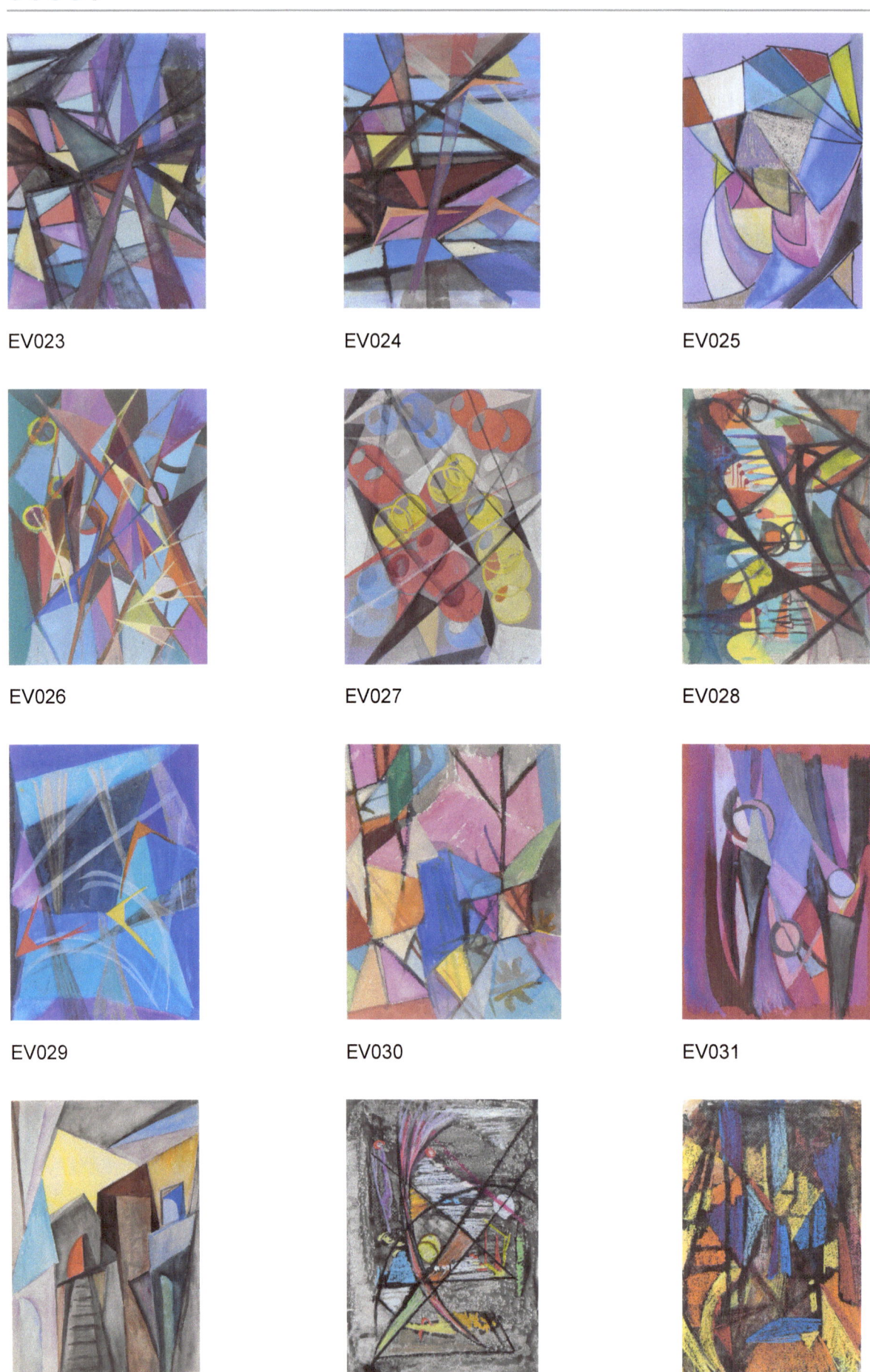

EV023

EV024

EV025

EV026

EV027

EV028

EV029

EV030

EV031

EV032

EV033

EV034

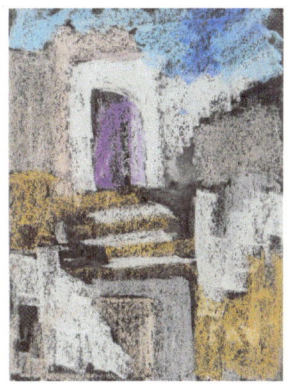
EV035

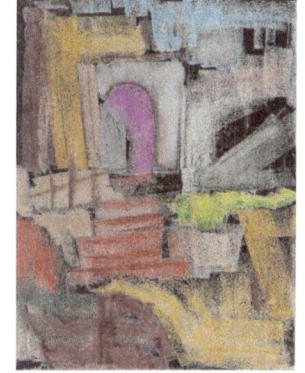
EV036

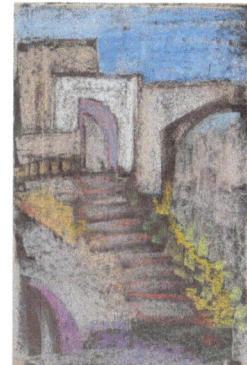
EV037

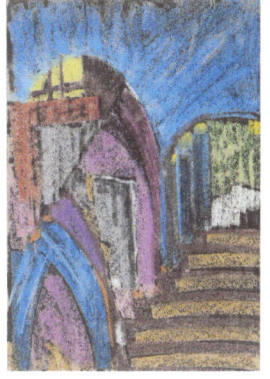
EV038

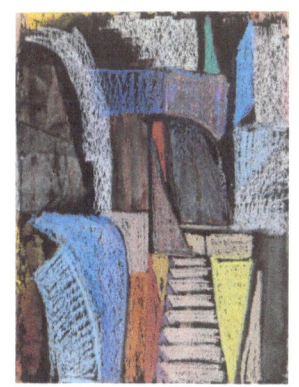
EV039

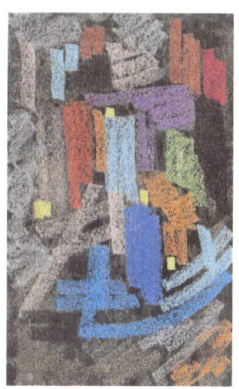
EV040

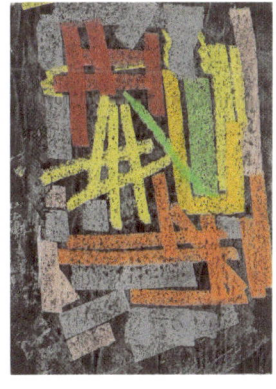
EV041

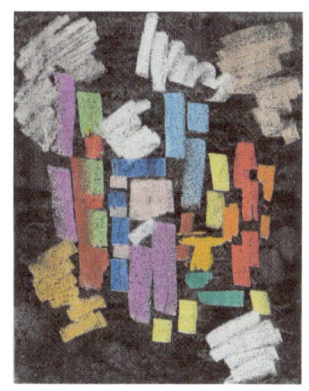
EV042

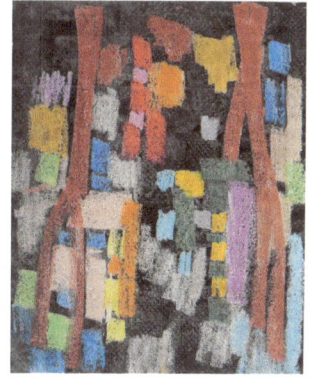
EV043

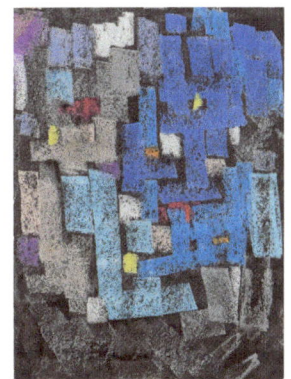
EV044

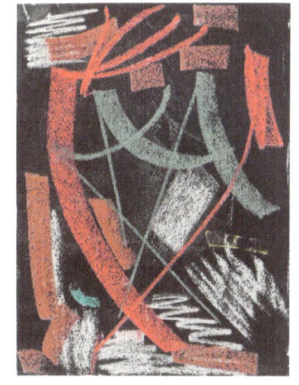
EV045

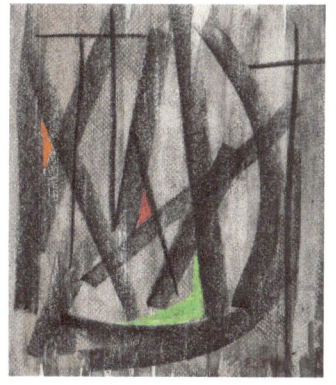
EV046

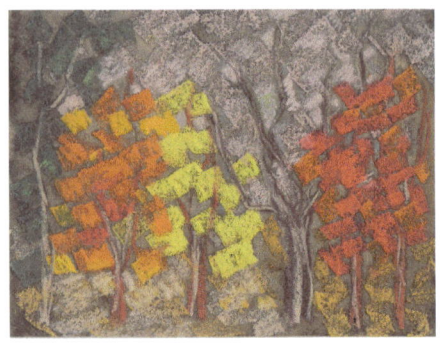
EV047

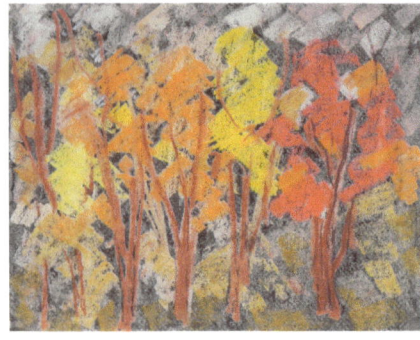
EV048

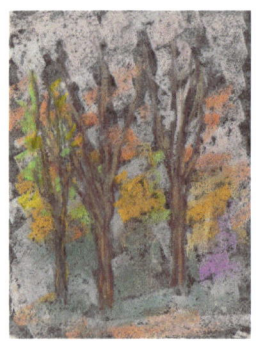
EV049

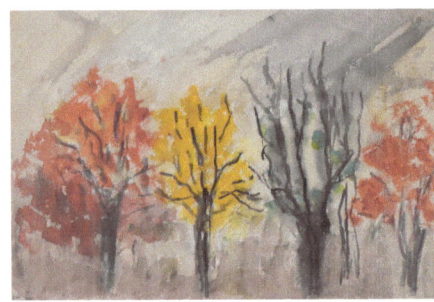
EV050

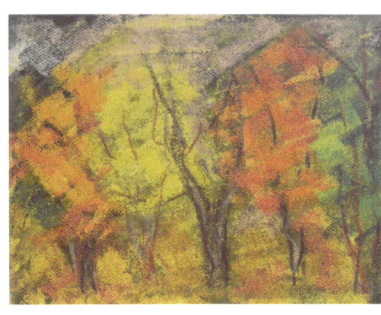
EV051

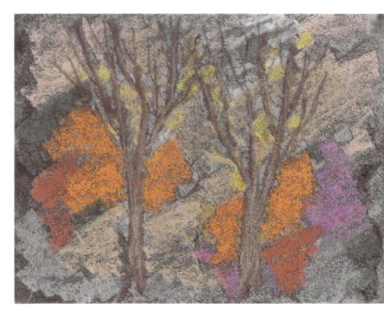
EV052

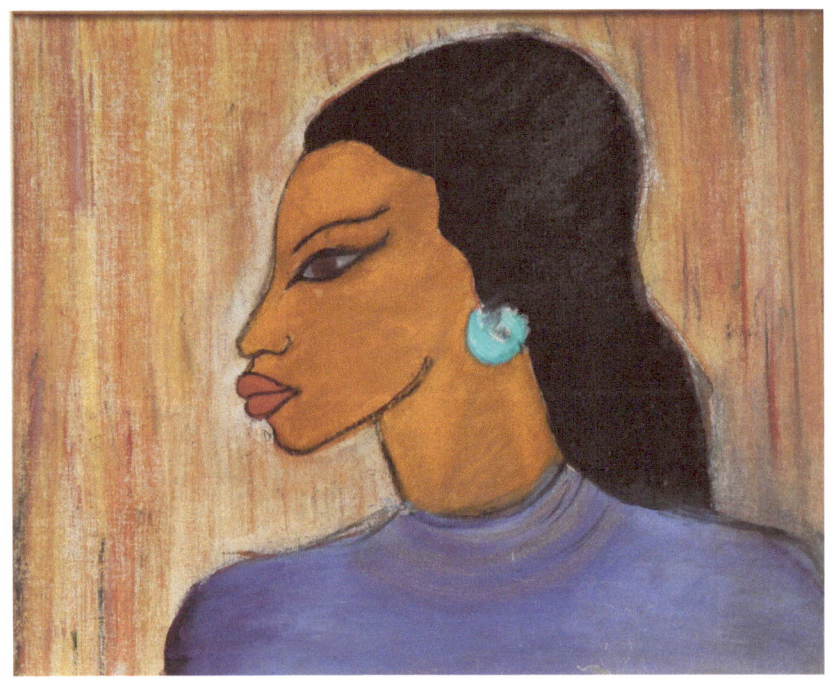
EV053

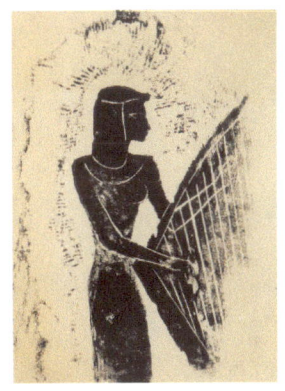

EV054

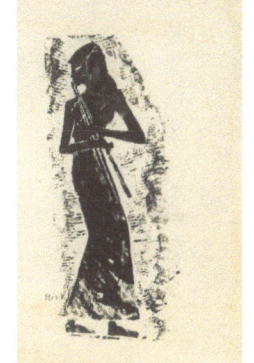

EV055

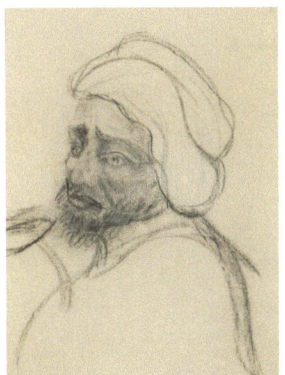

EV056

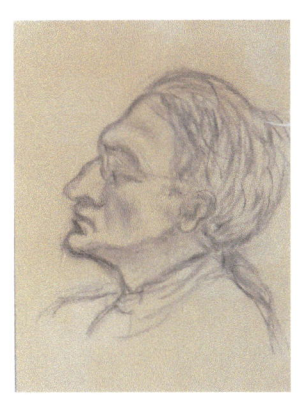

EV057

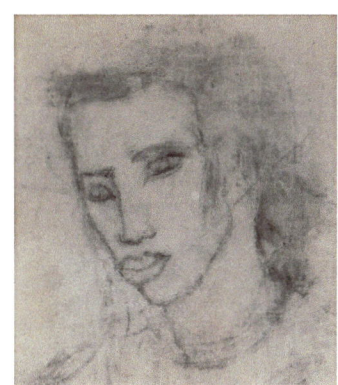

EV058

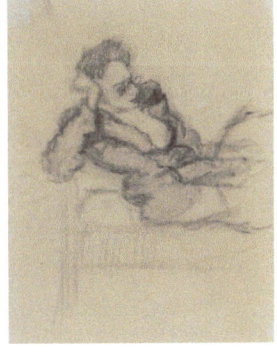

EV059

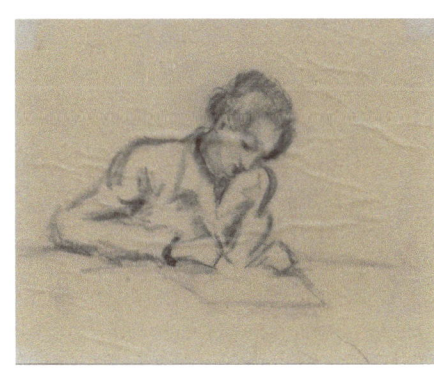

EV060

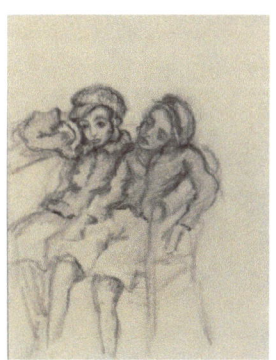

EV061

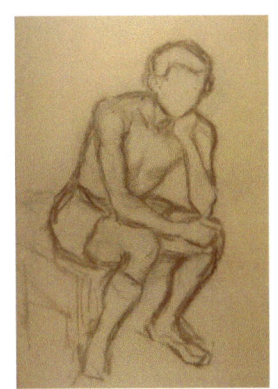

EV062

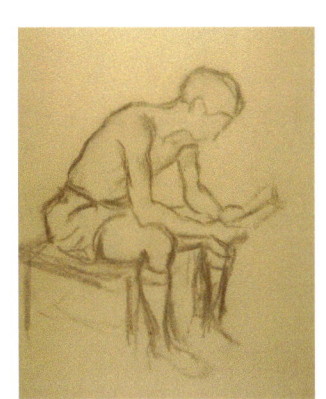

EV063

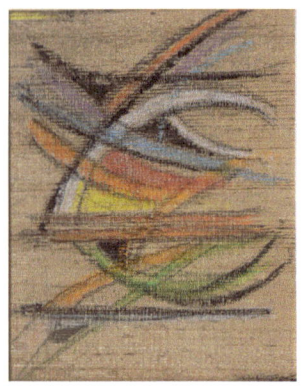
EV064

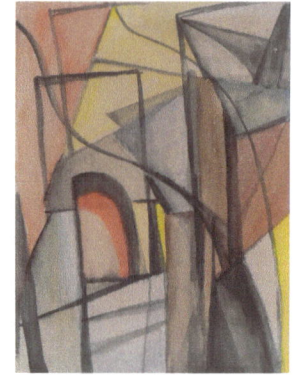
EV065

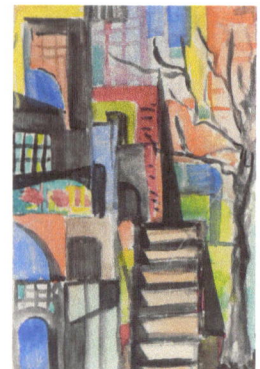
EV066

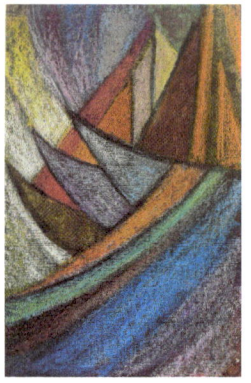
EV067

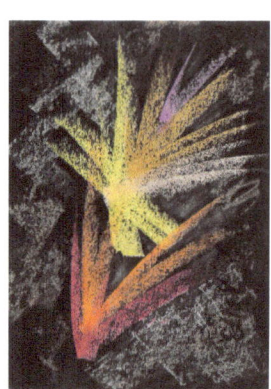
EV068

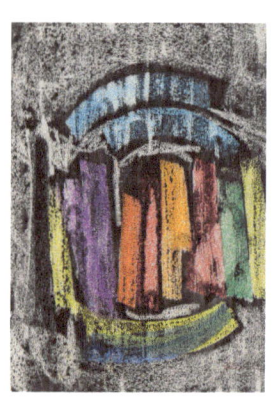
EV069

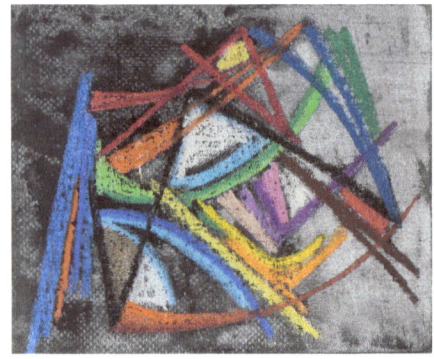
EV070

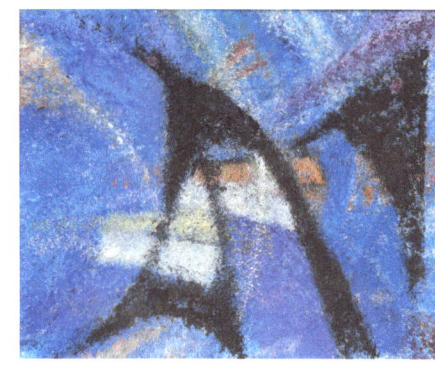
EV071

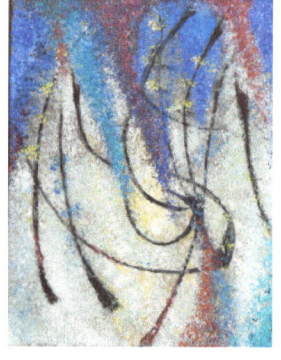
EV072

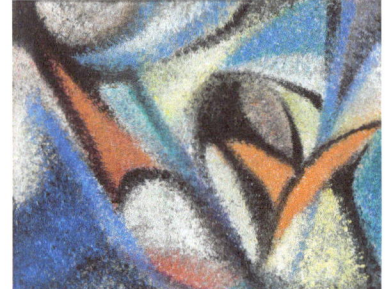
EV073

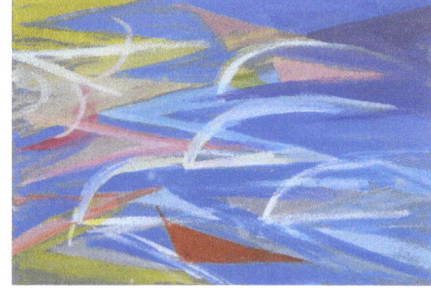
EV074

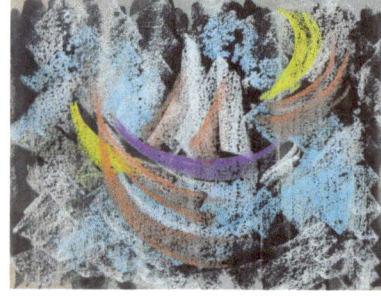
EV075

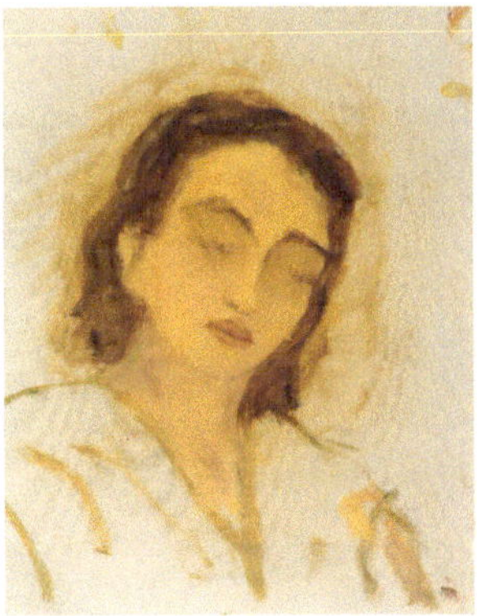

EV076 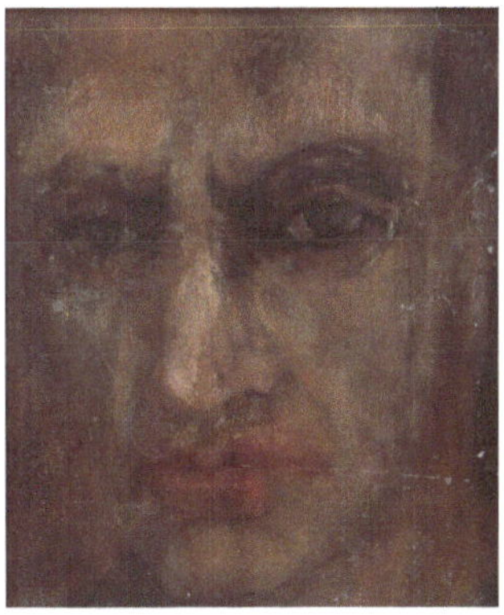   EV077 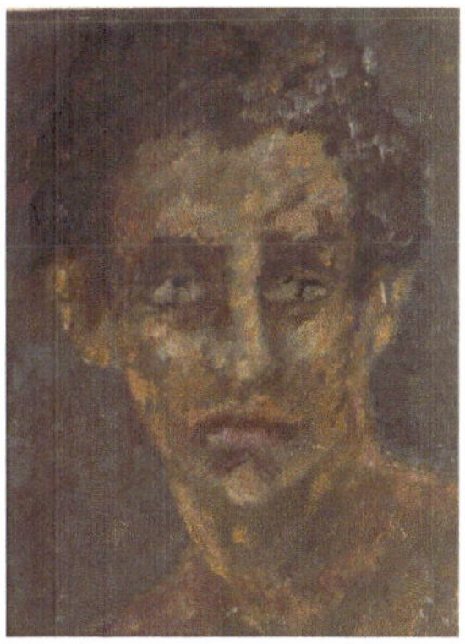   EV078

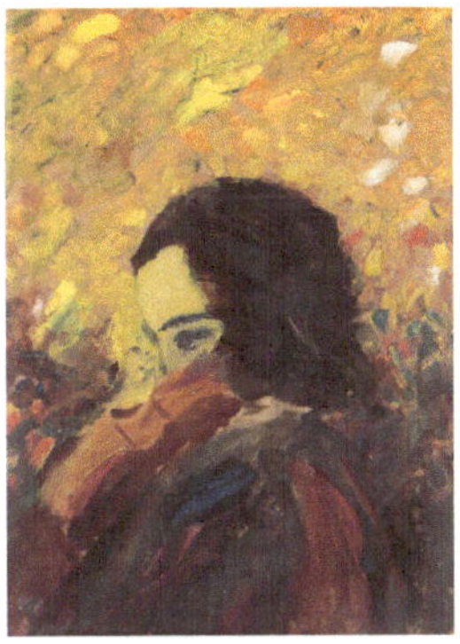

EV079 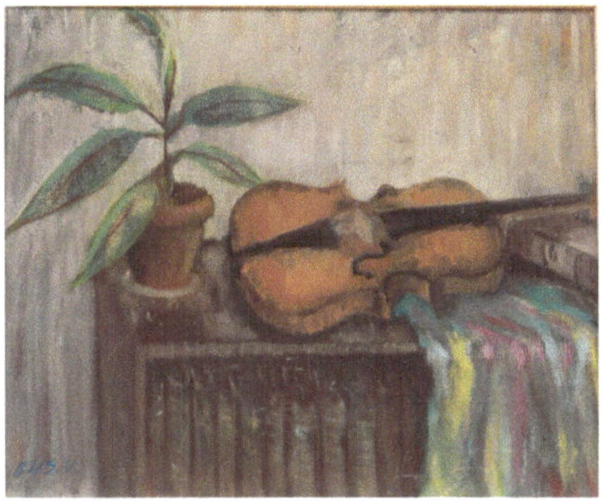   EV080 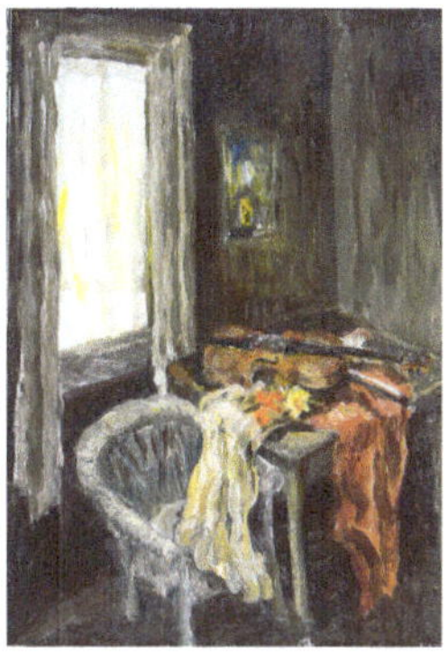   EV081

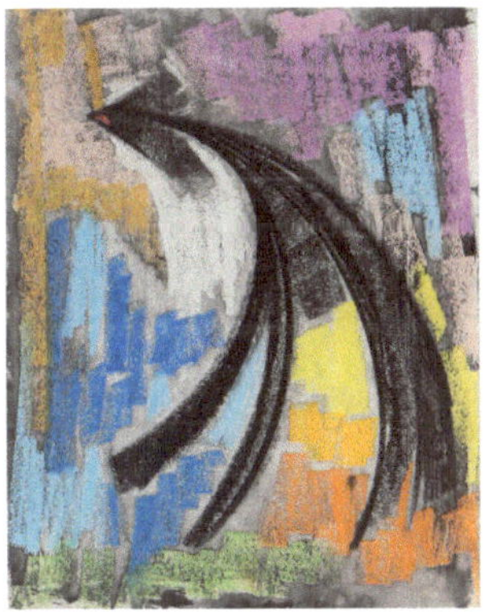

EV082 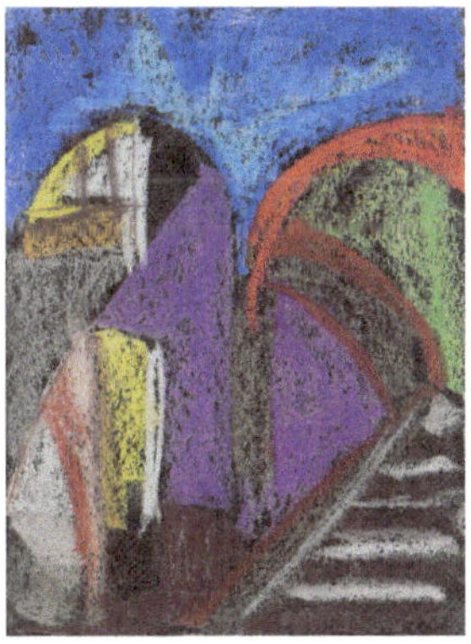   EV083 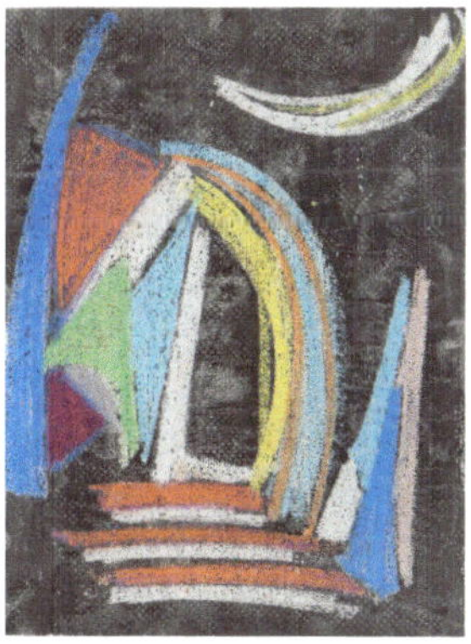   EV084

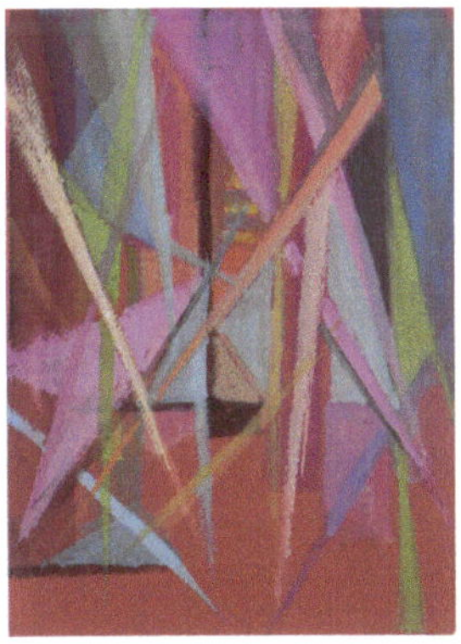

EV085 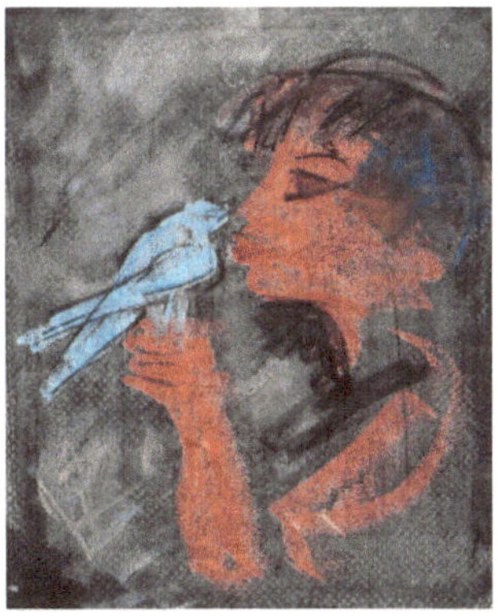   EV086 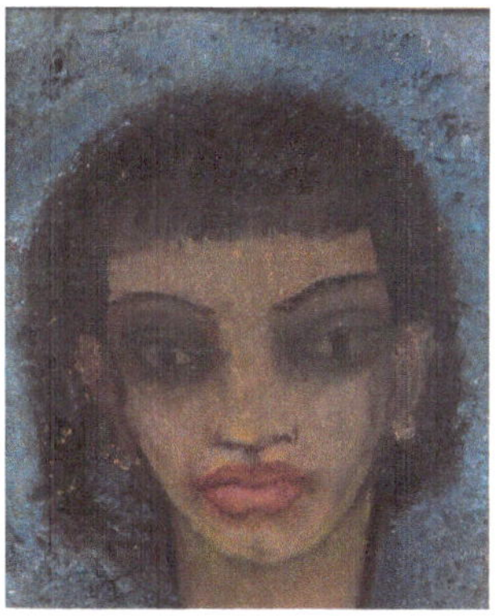   EV087

15

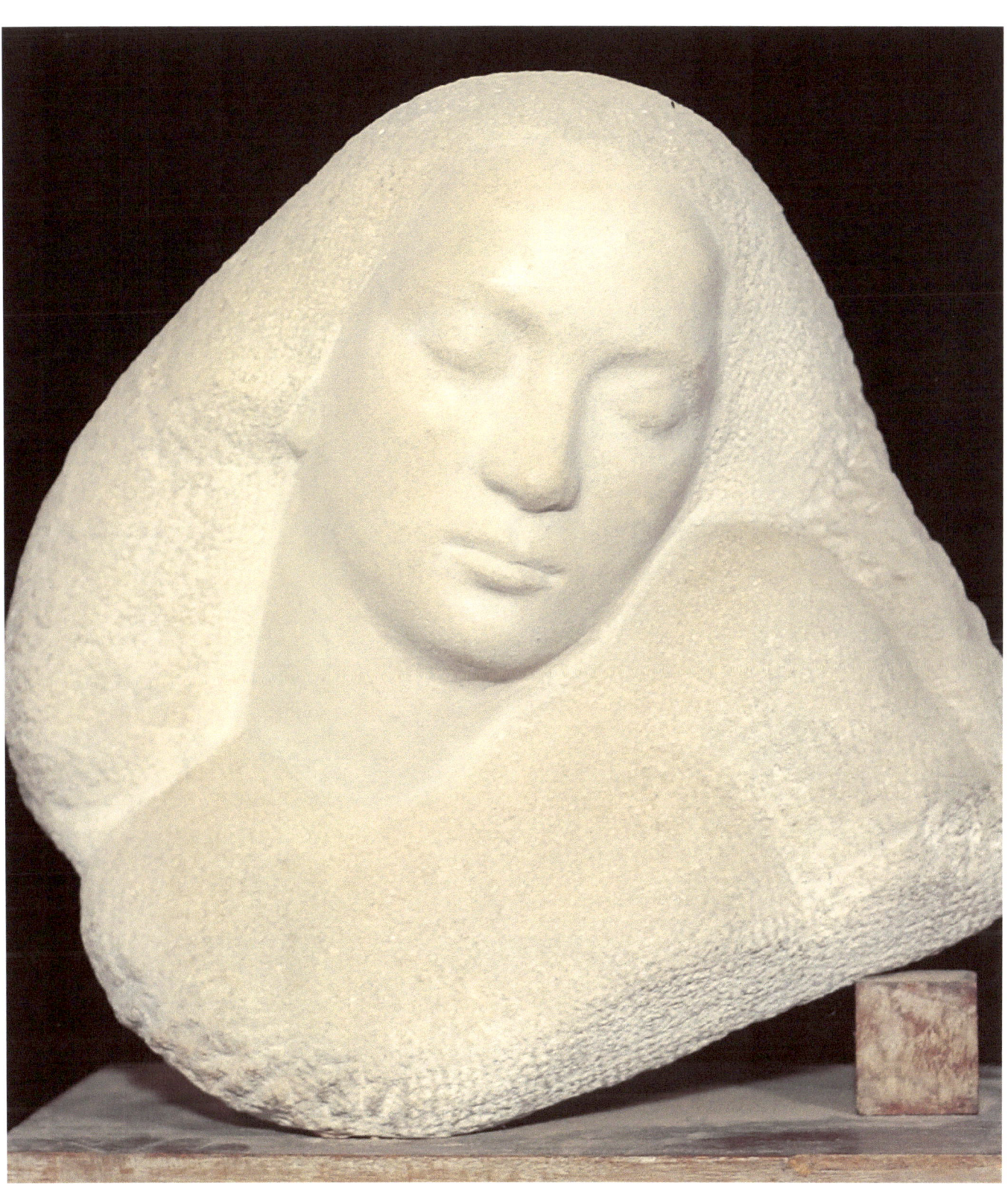

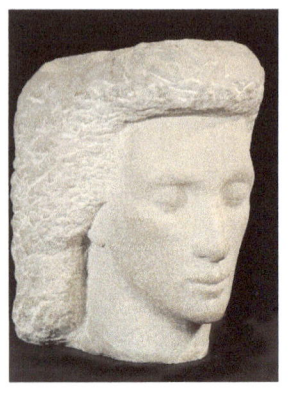 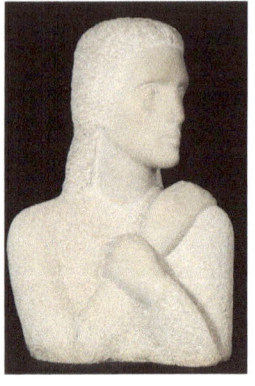 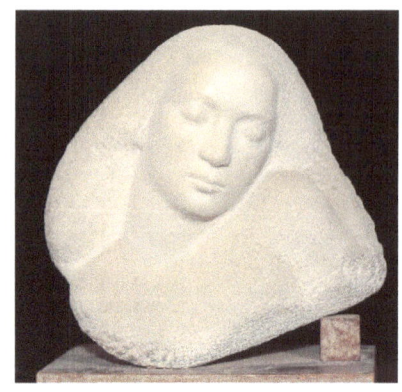

SC002   SC003

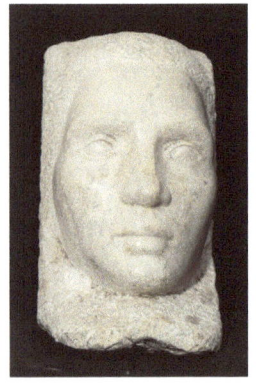 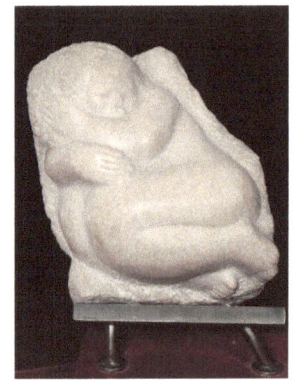 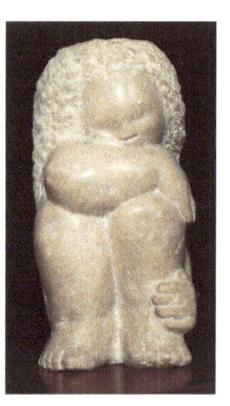

SC004   SC005   SC006

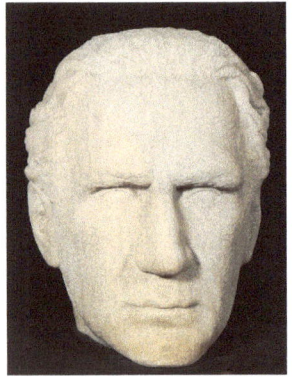

SC007

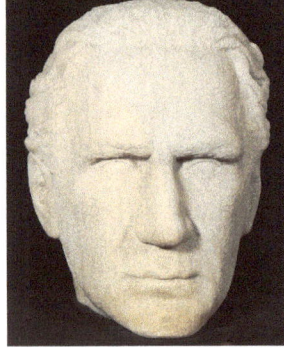 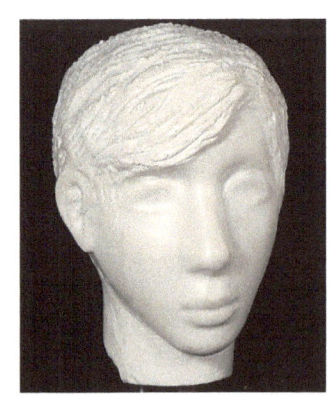 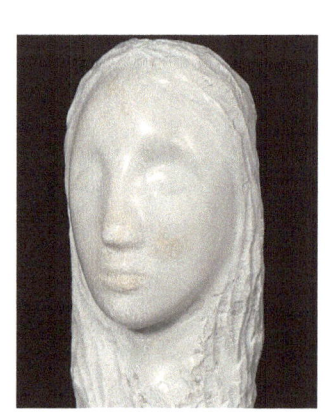

SC008   SC009   SC010

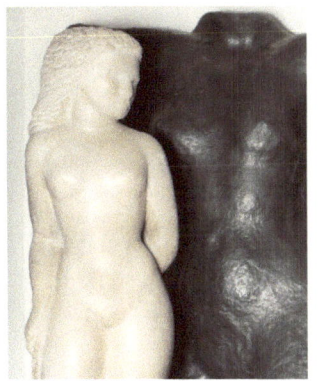
SC011

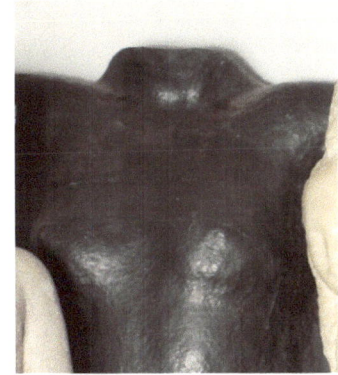
SC012

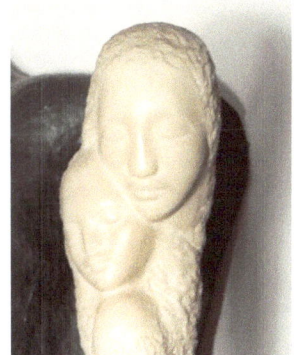
SC013

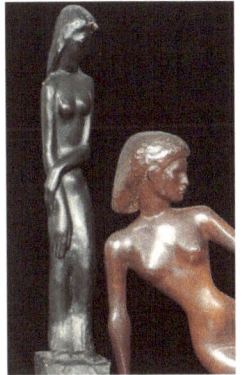
SC014

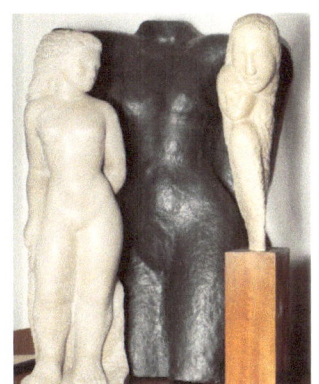
SC015

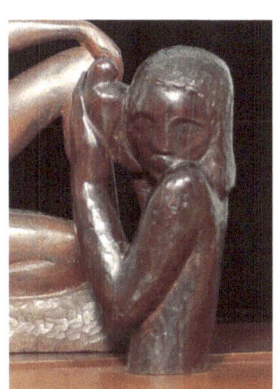
SC016

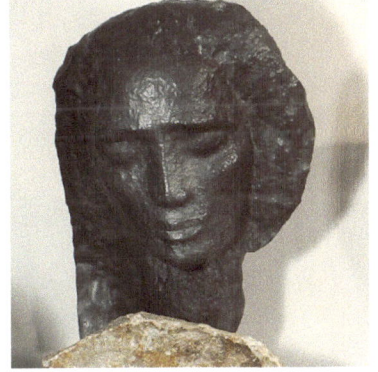
SC017

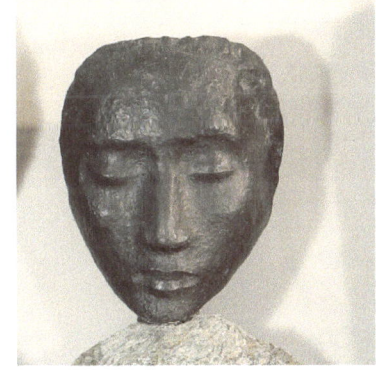
SC018

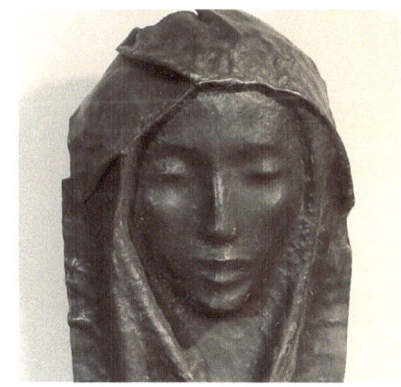
SC019

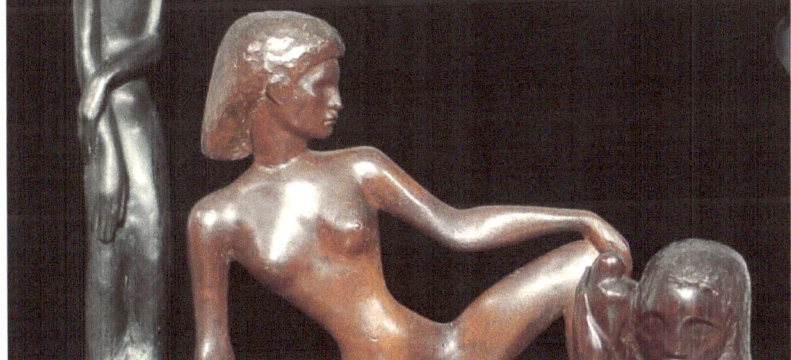
SC020

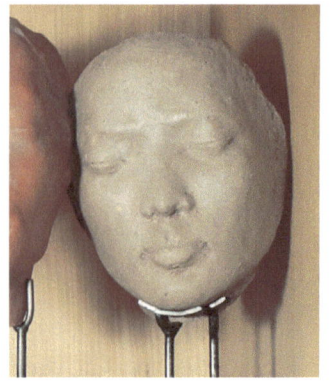

SC021

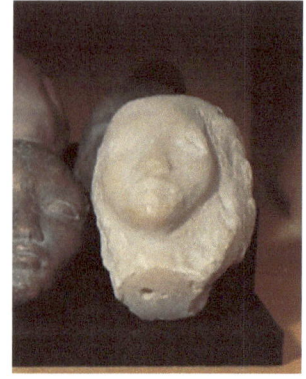

SC022

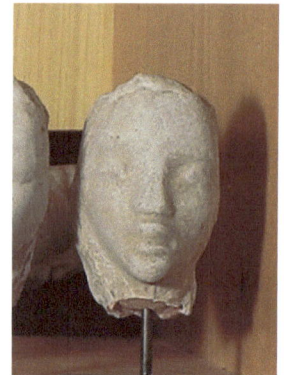

SC023

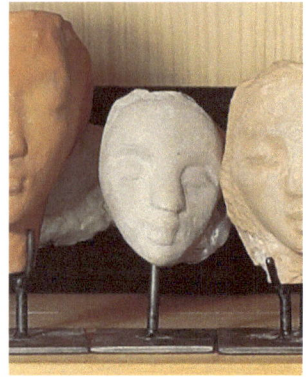

SC024

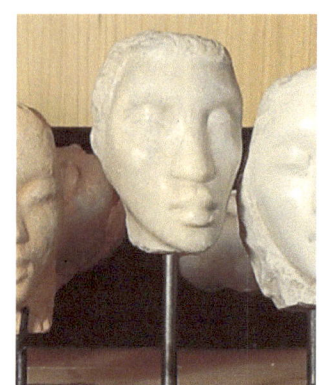

SC025

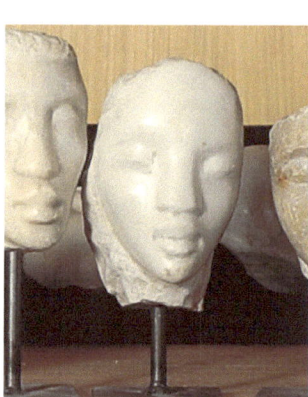

SC026

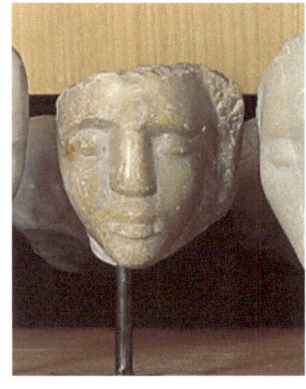

SC027

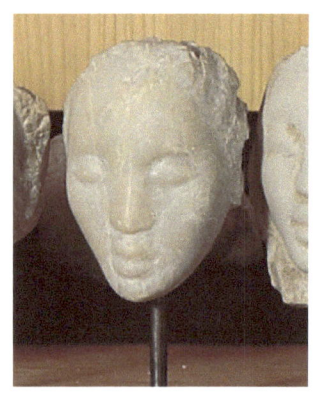

SC028

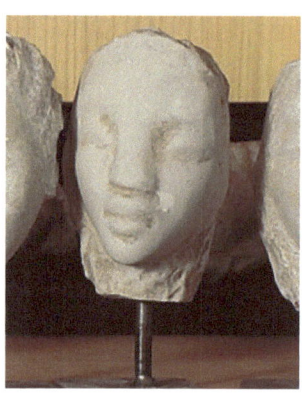

SC029

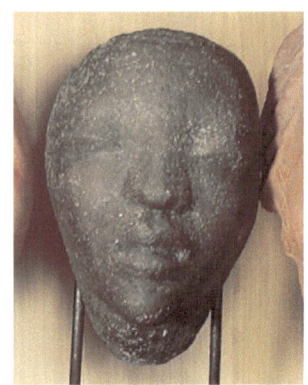

SC030

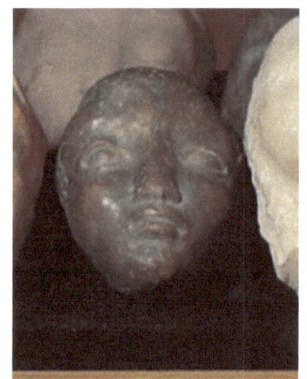

SC031

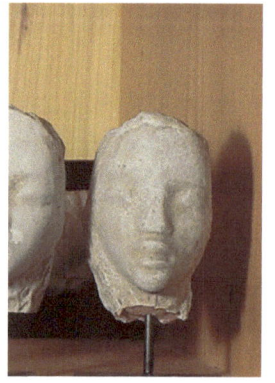

SC032

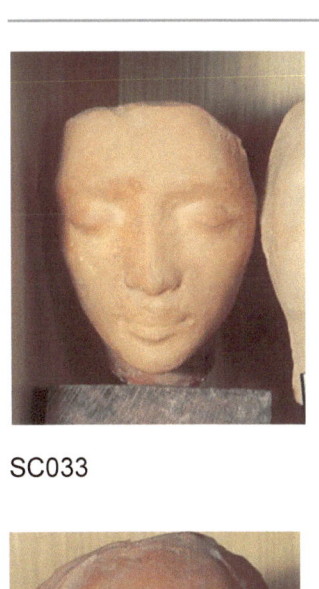
SC033

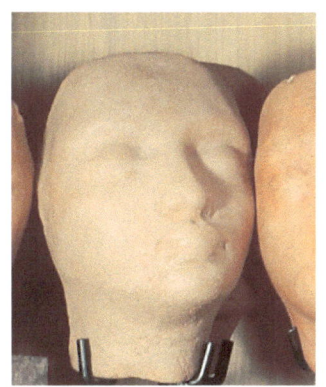
SC034

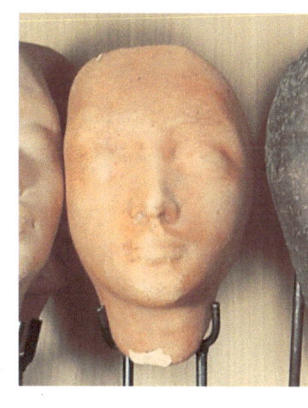
SC035

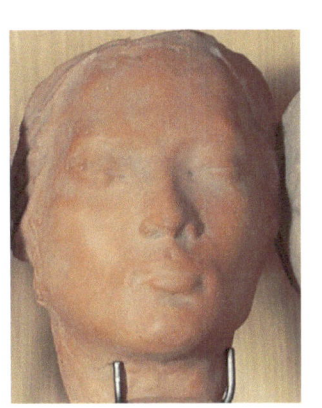
SC036

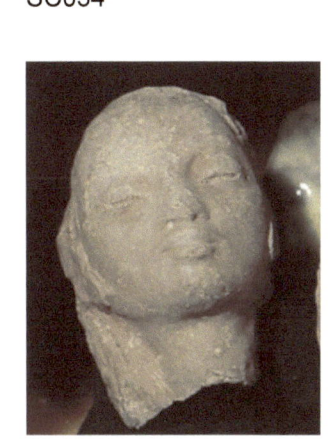
SC037

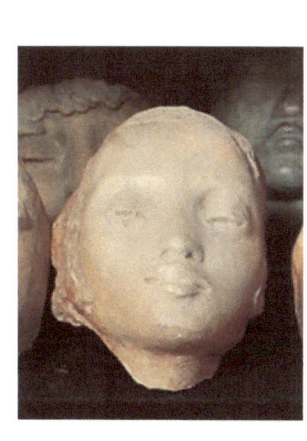
SC038

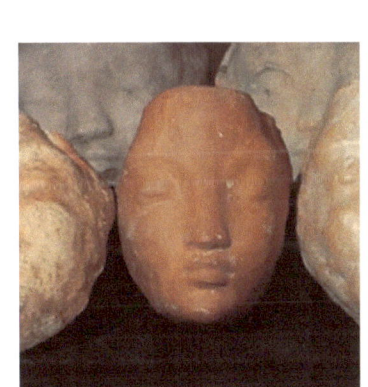
SC039

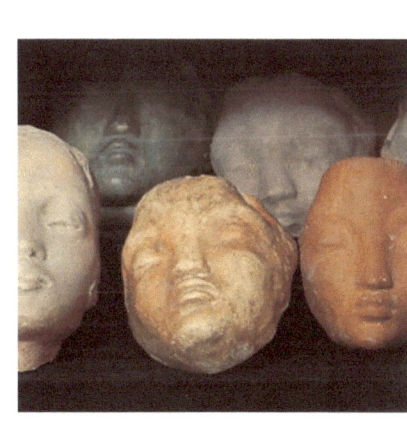
SC040

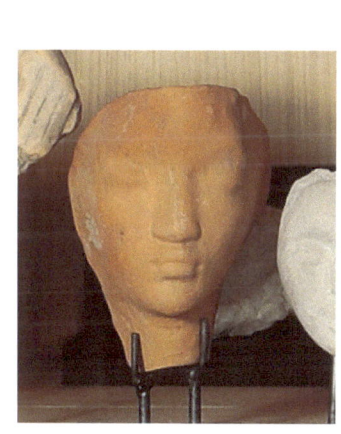
SC041

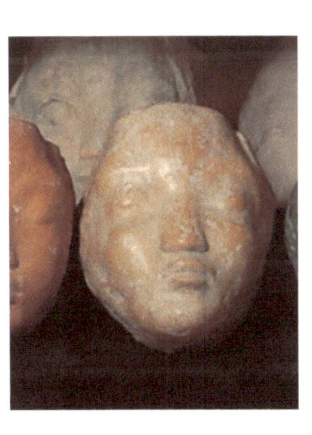
SC042

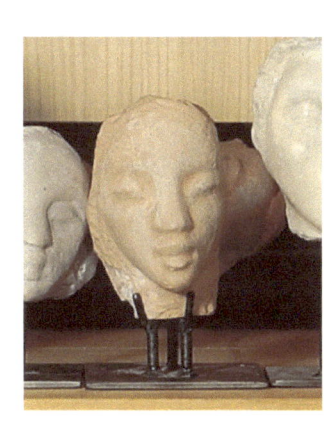
SC043

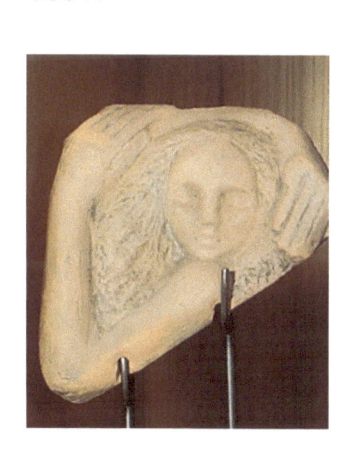
SC044

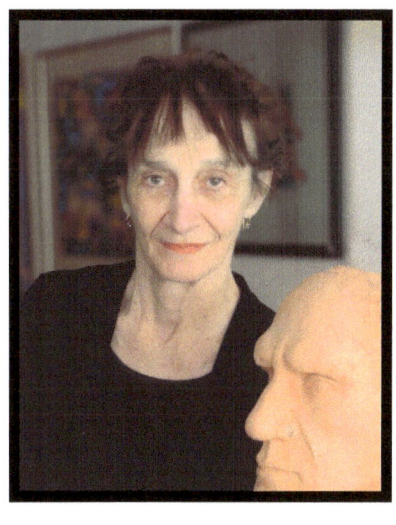

Dr. Ruth Velikovsky Sharon

Dr. Ruth Velikovsky Sharon learned at the desk of her distinguished father, Dr. Immanuel Velikovsky, a prominent psychiatrist and eminent man of science whose genius engaged even the mind of his friend and contemporary, Albert Einstein.

At the same time, sitting in the room with her mother's (Elis Velikovsky) works, listening to Mozart, she had herself inspired artistically.

Dr. Sharon received B.A and M.A. degrees from New York University and a Ph.D. from the Union Institute and University. She is a graduate of the Center for Modern Psychoanalytic Studies and a certified psychoanalyst.

She taught arts and crafts at the Sharon Studio in Princeton from 1955 to 1974, which enjoyed a well deserved reputation for originating new concepts of teaching in this field to children, with emphasis on liberating creativity and undisturbed self-expression.

She has exhibited in central New Jersey, including the New Jersey State Museum, and also in New York in The Pen and Brush.

She works with pen and india ink, with watercolors, on leather, silk, linen, burlap and blotter paper. Her favorite themes are the violin (because of her mother), Jerusalem (where she was born) and birds (simply because of their shape).

Her One-Woman Shows:

    1972 Artisan, Princeton, New Jersey

    1974 The Suzuki Gallery Kingston, New Jersey

    1976 Gallery 100 Princeton, New Jersey

    1987 The Pen and Brush, New York, New York

    1987 The Full House, Kingston, New Jersey

    1990 Williams Collection New Visions Gallery, Kingston, New Jersey

    1992 The Jewish Center, Sponsored by the Williams Collection, Princeton, New Jersey

    1998 The Verdge, Princeton, New Jersey

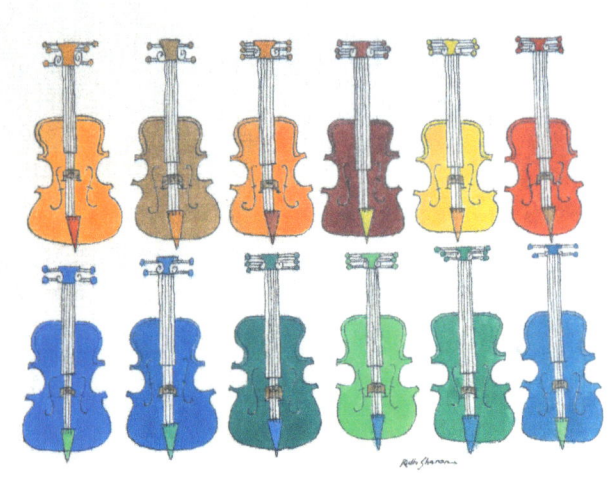

RS001

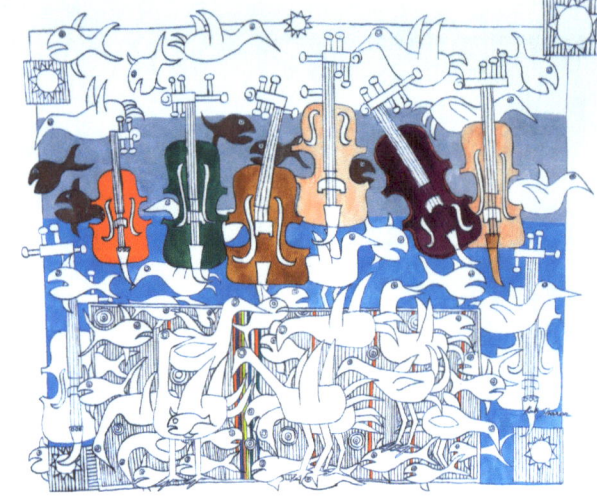

RS002

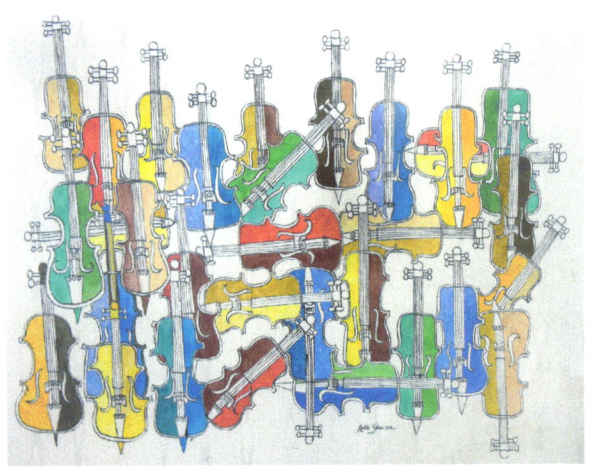

RS003

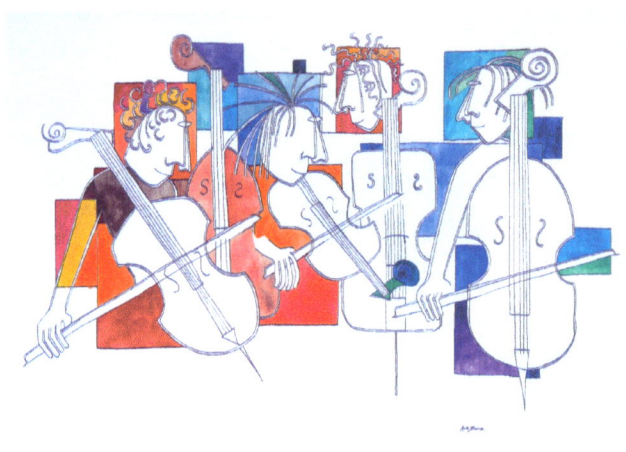

RS004

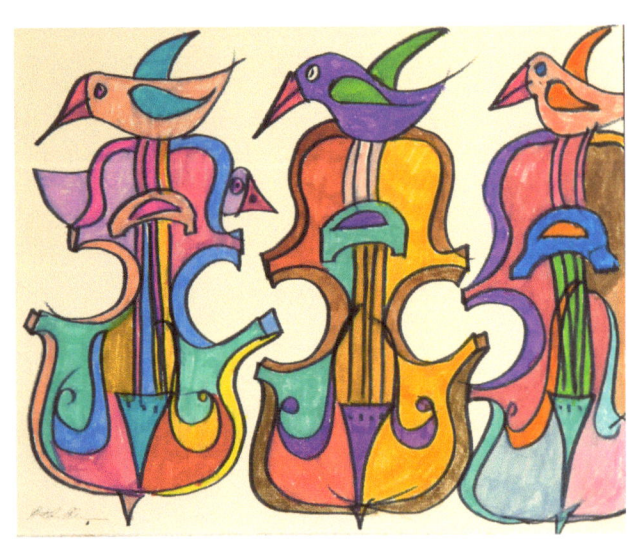

RS005

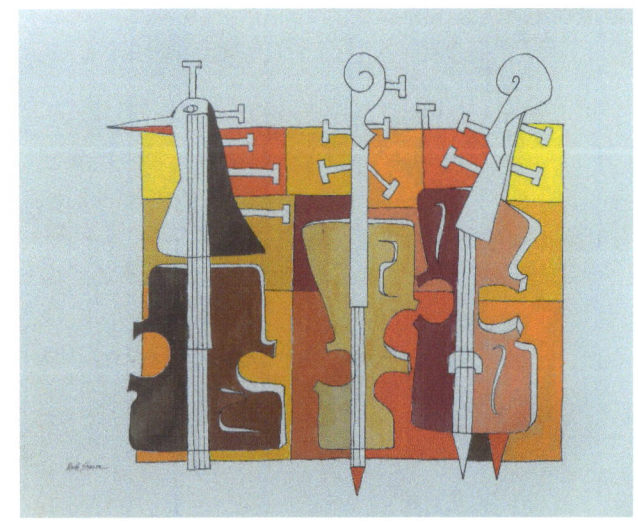

RS006

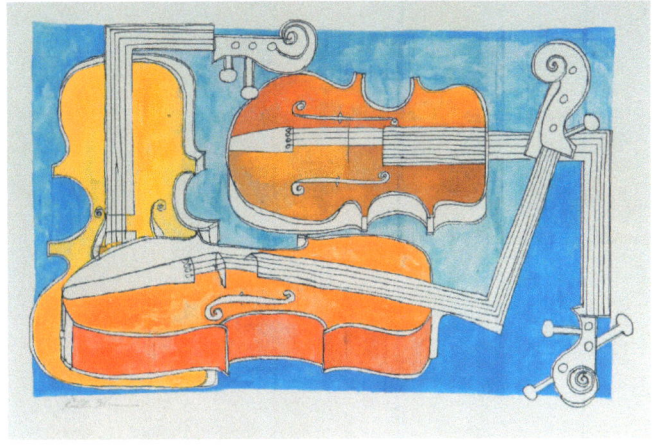

RS007

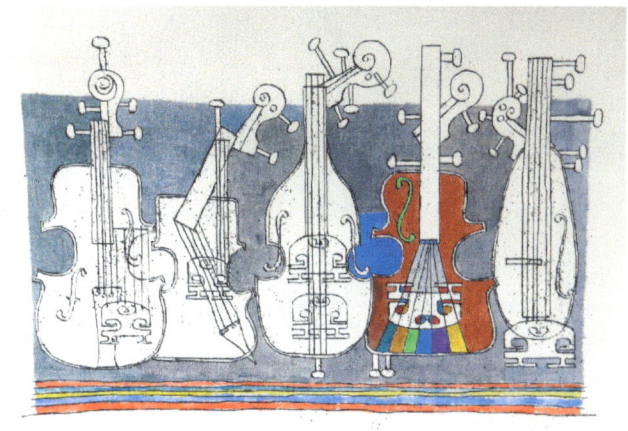

RS008

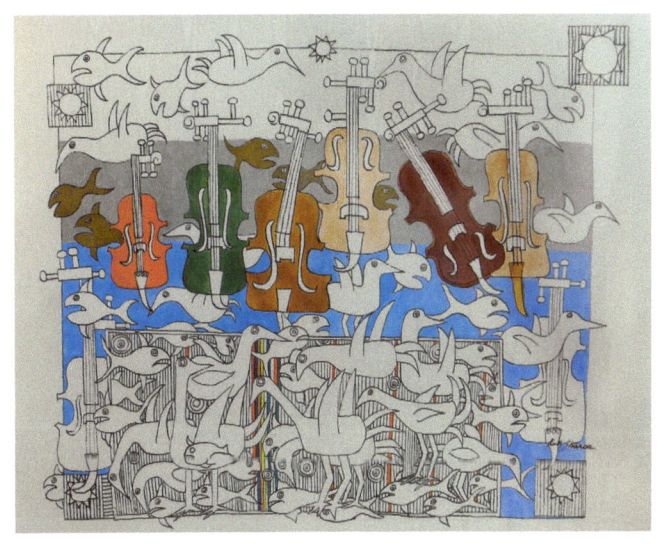

RS009

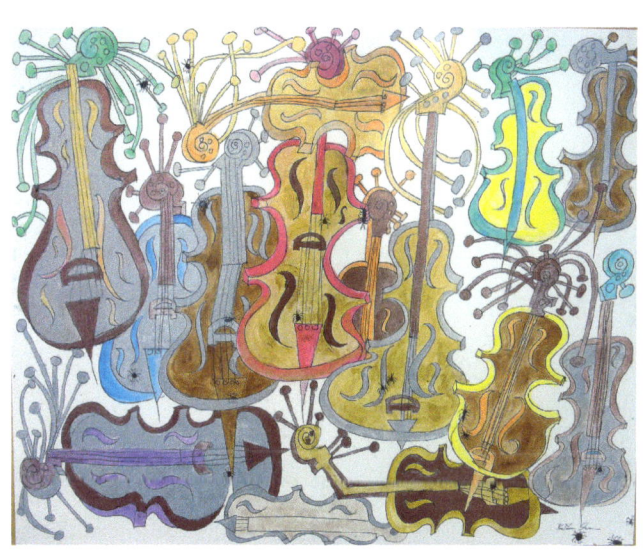

RS010

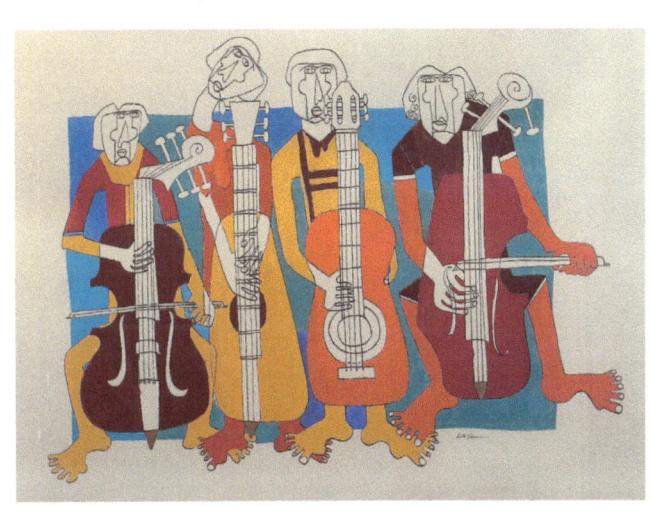

RS011

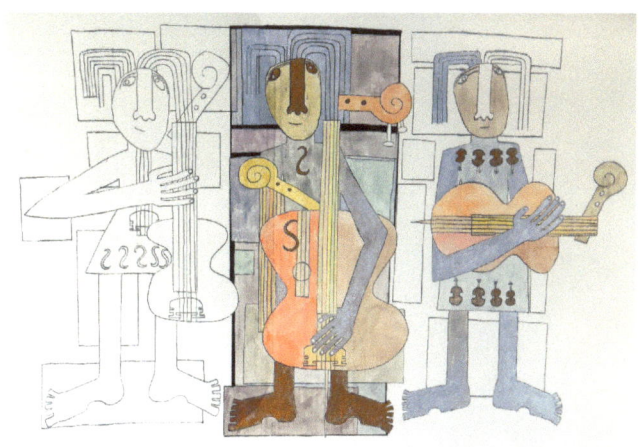

RS012

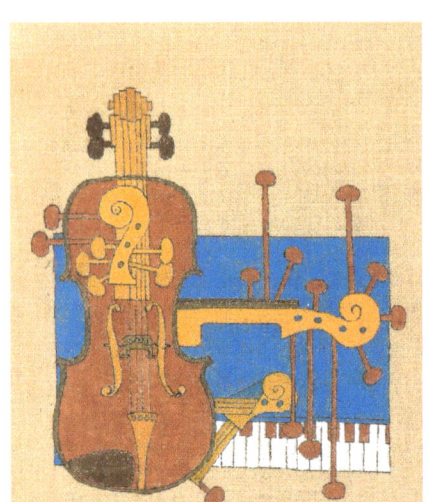

RS013

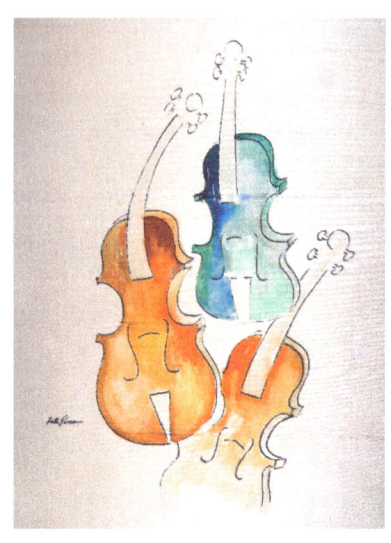

RS014

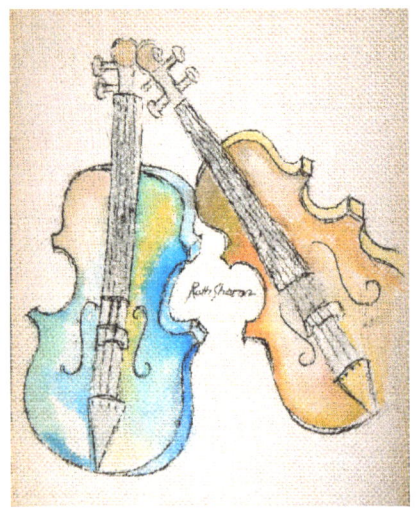

RS015

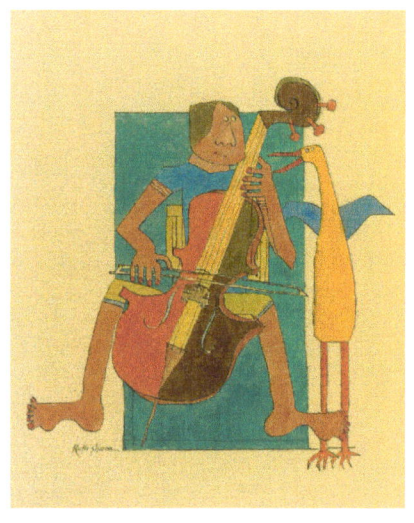

RS016

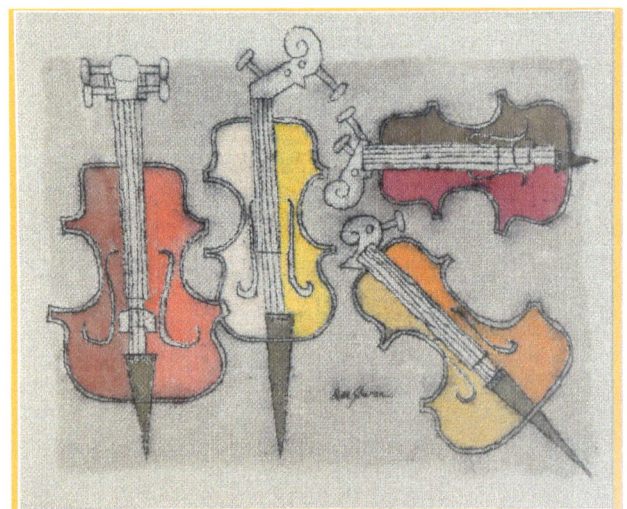

RS017

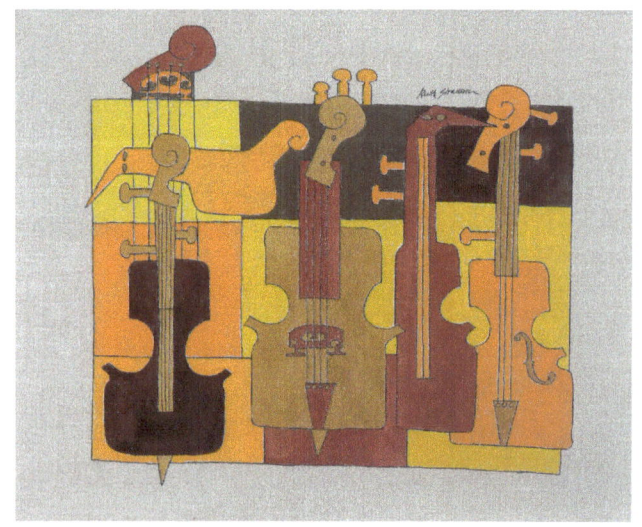

RS018

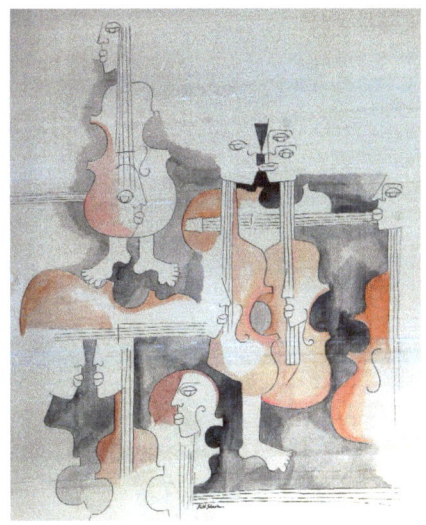

RS019

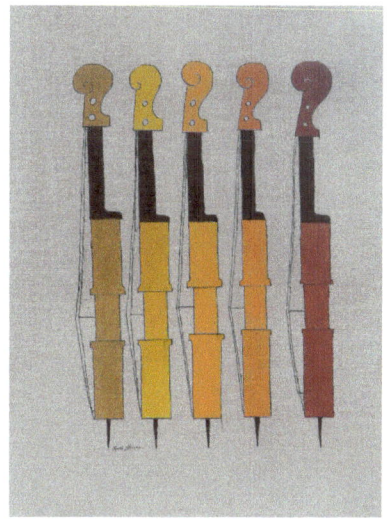

RS020

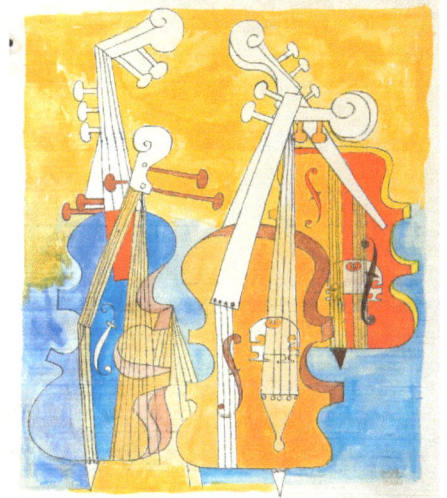

RS021

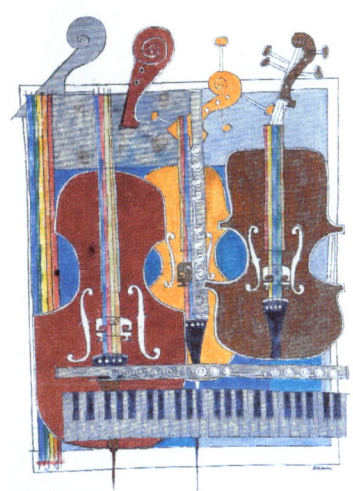

RS022

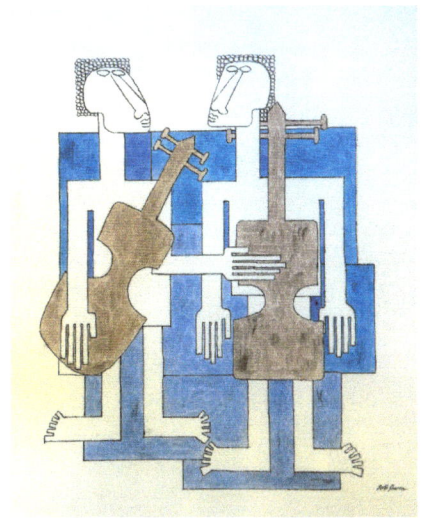

RS023

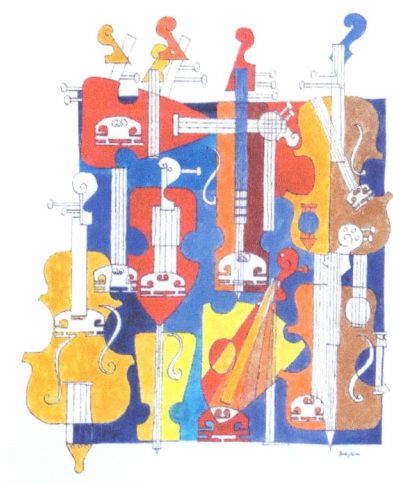

RS024

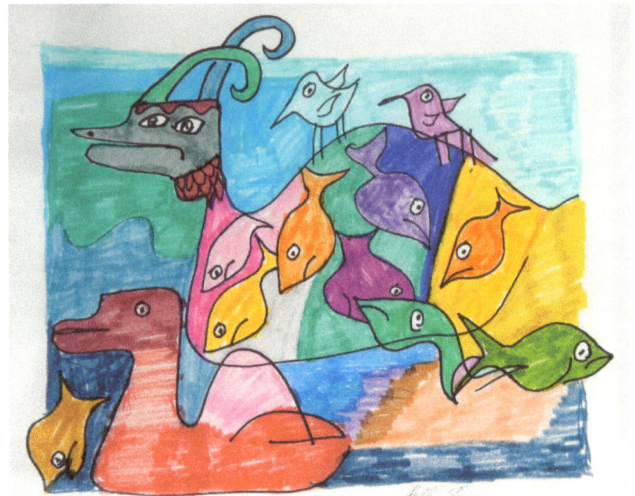
RS025

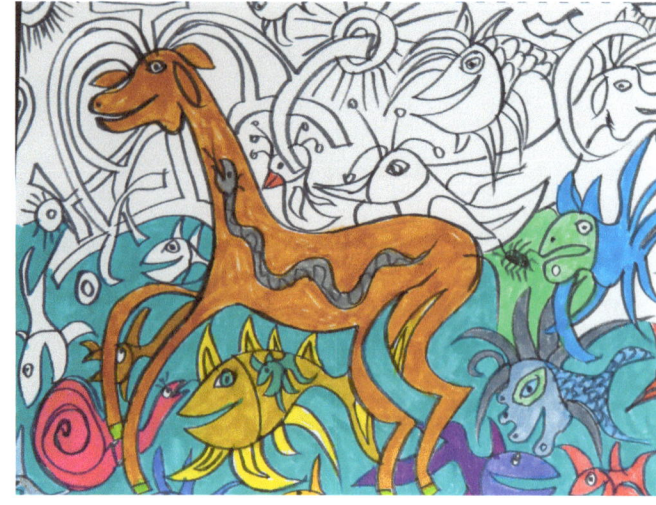
RS026

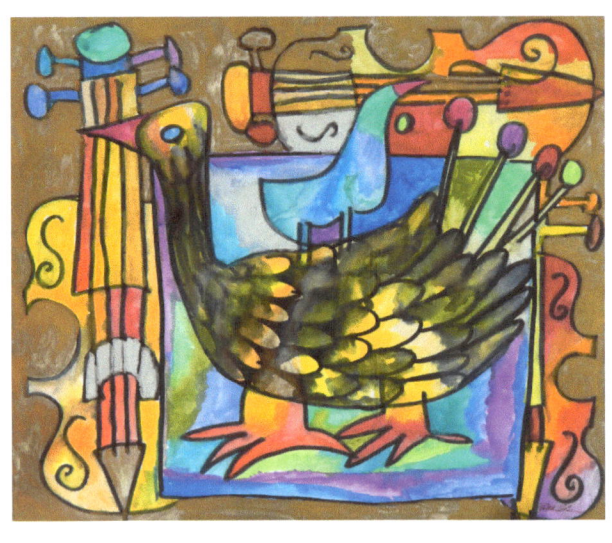
RS027

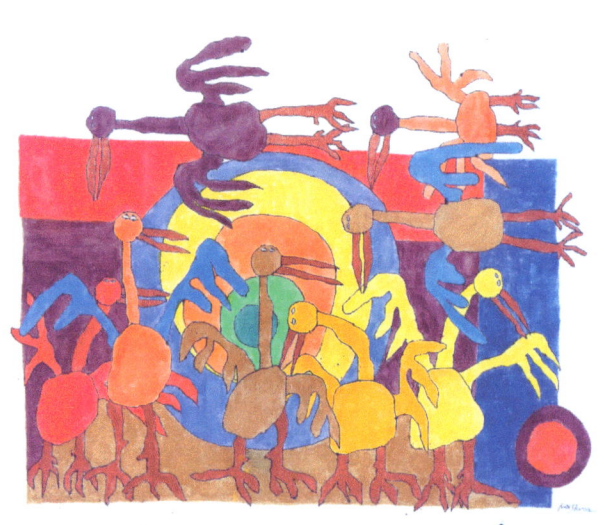
RS028

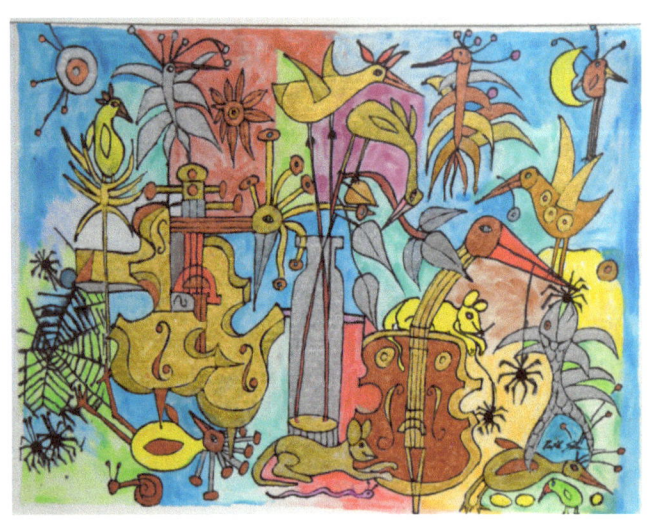
RS029

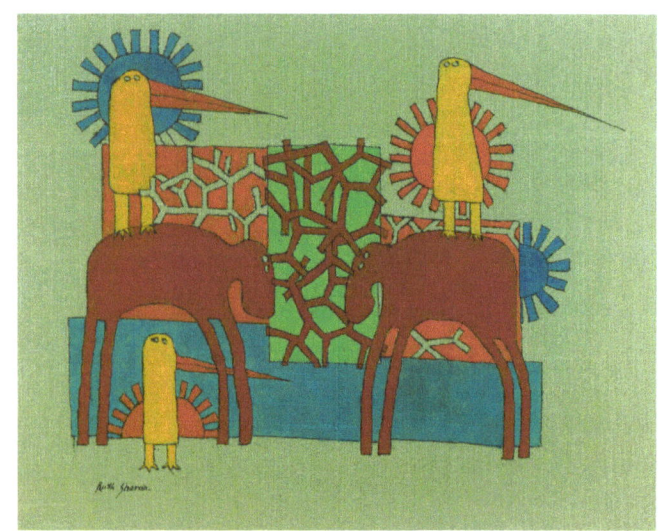
RS030

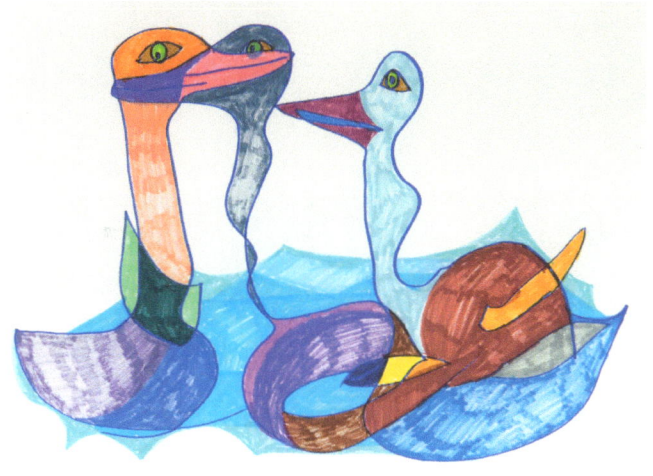

RS031

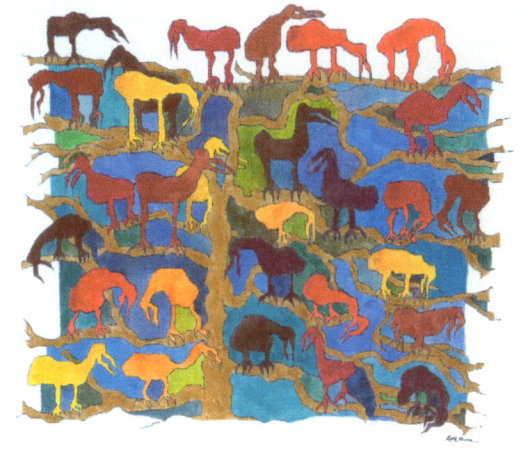

RS032

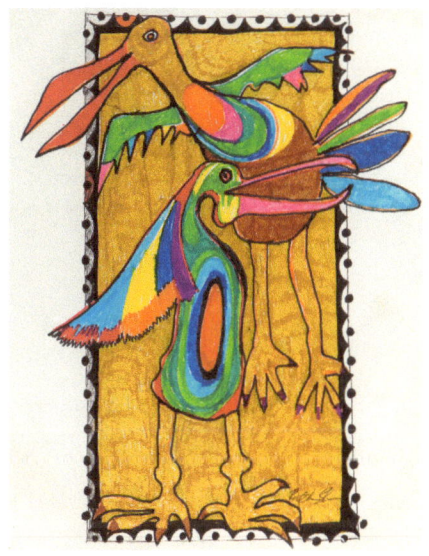

RS033

RS034

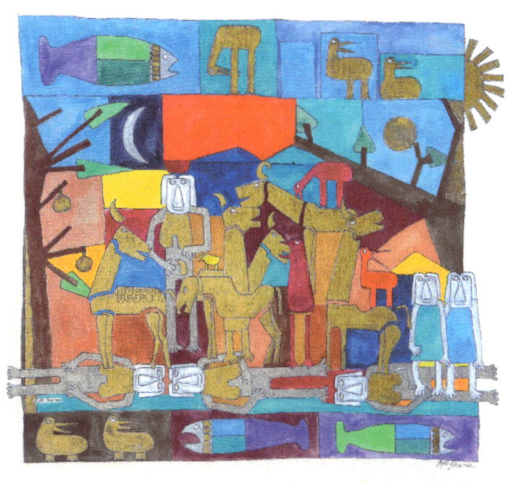

RS035

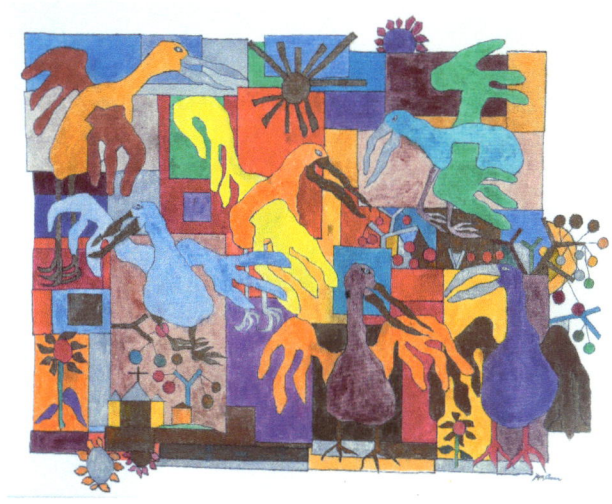

RS036

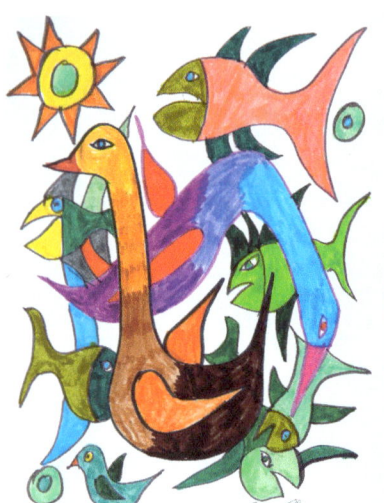

RS037

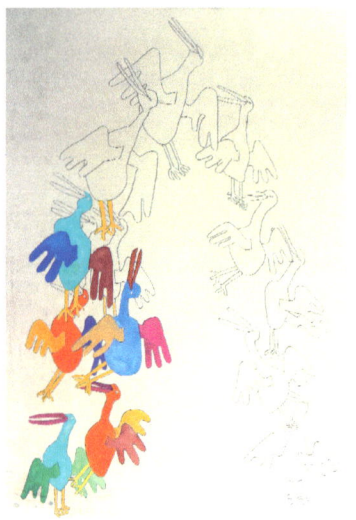

RS038

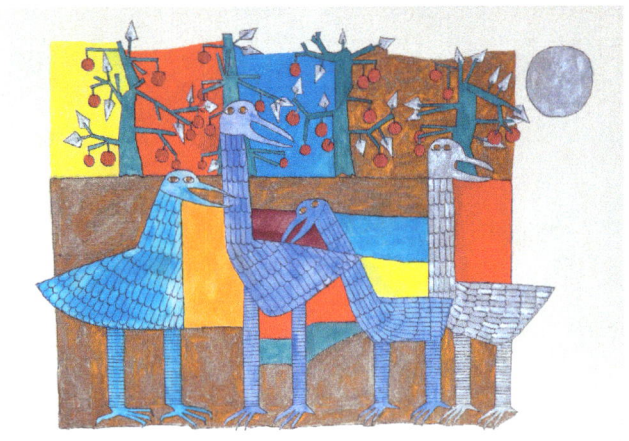

RS039

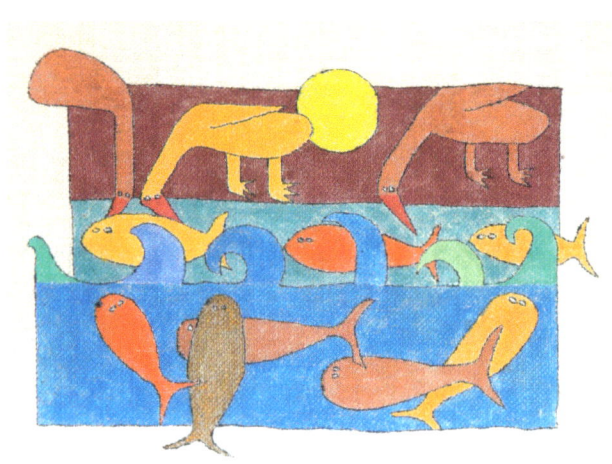

RS040

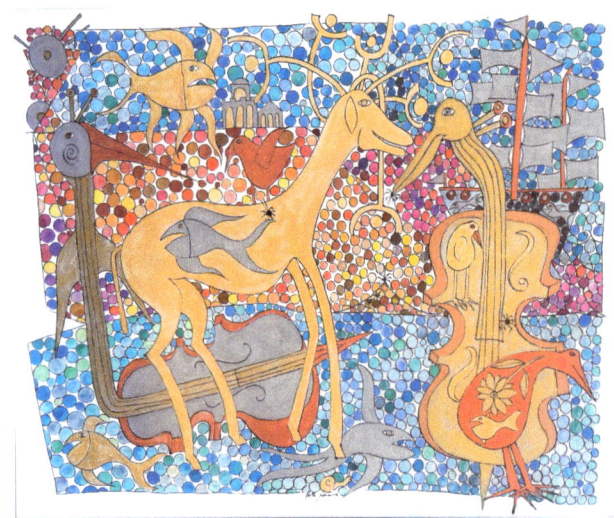

RS041

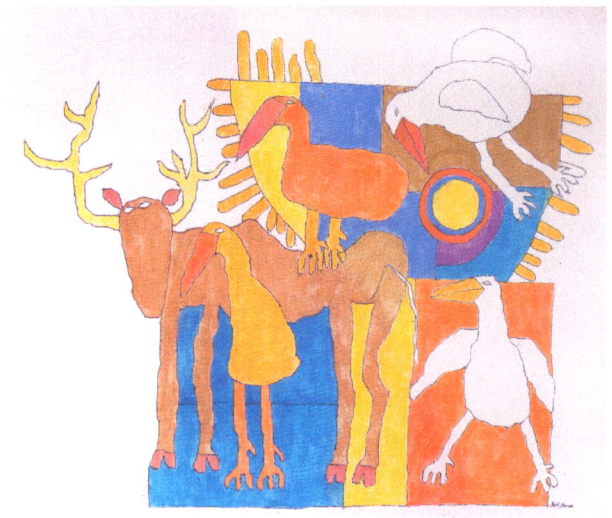

RS042

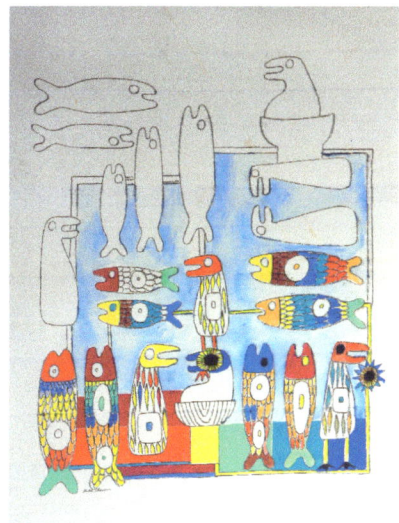

RS043

RS044

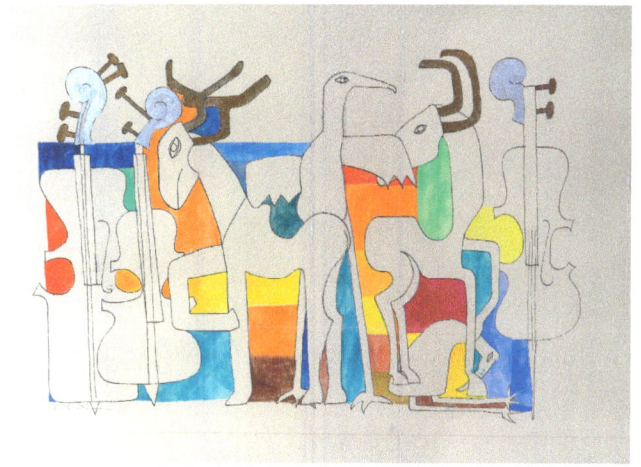

RS045

RS046

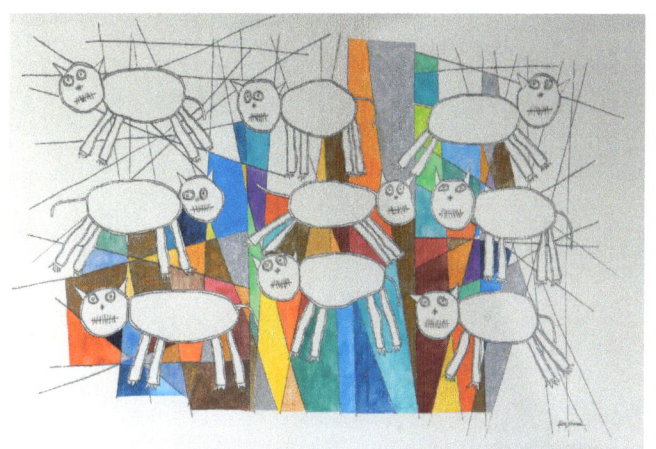

RS047

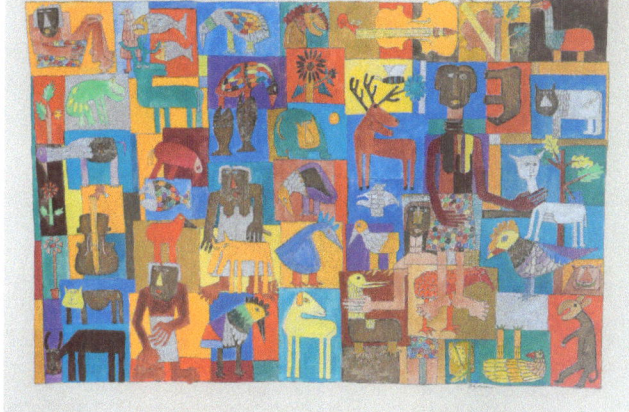

RS048

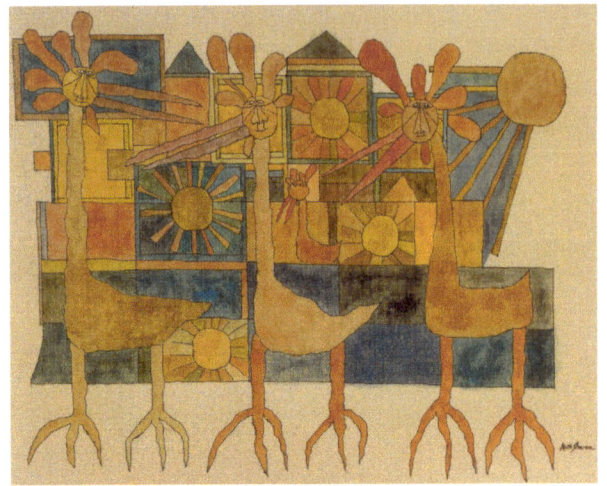
RS049

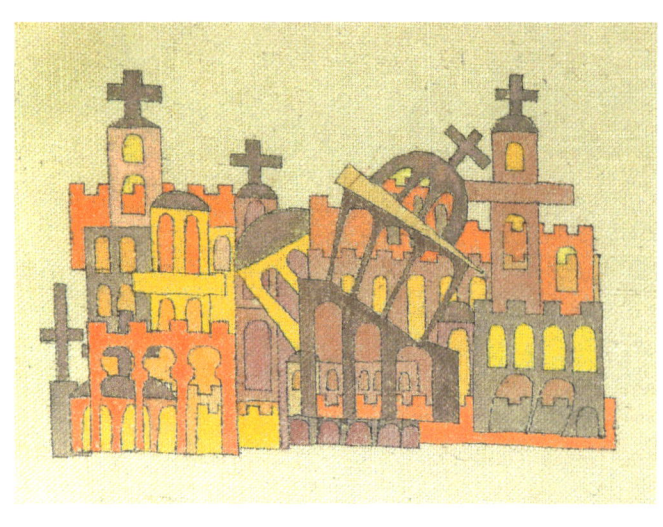
RS050

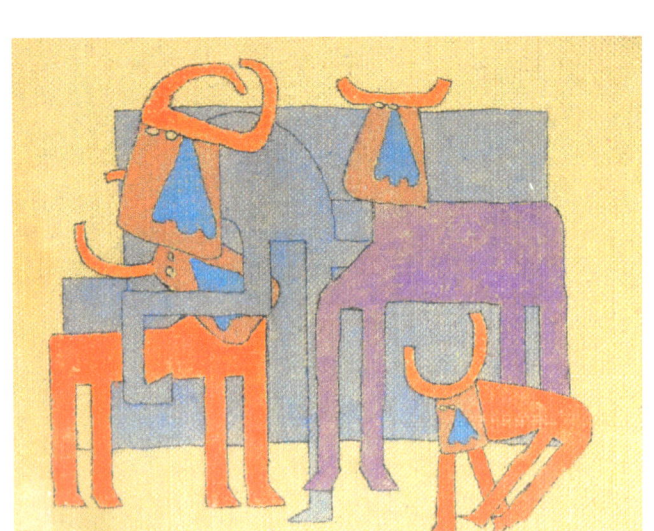
RS051

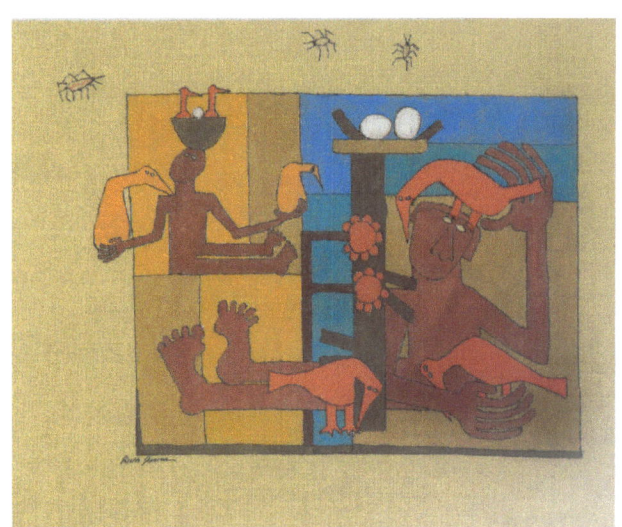
RS052

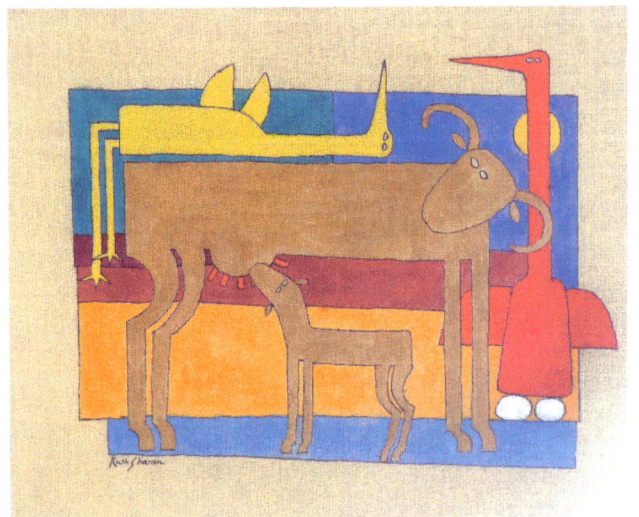
RS053

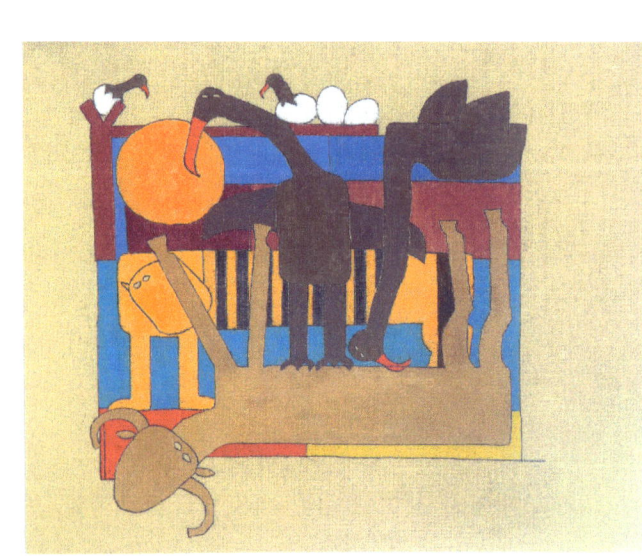
RS054

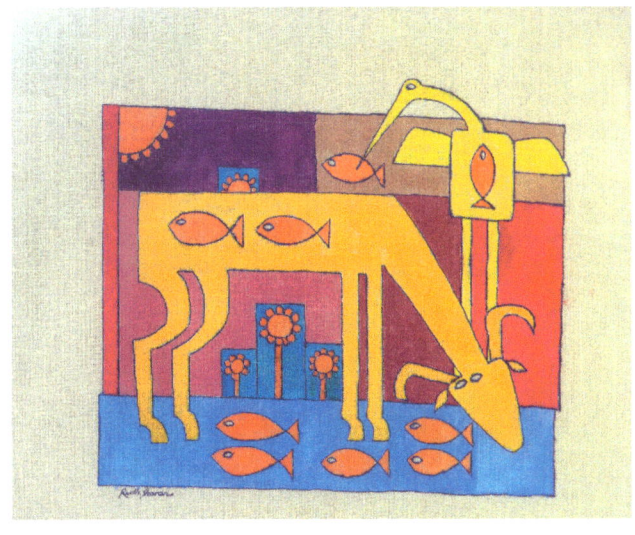

RS055

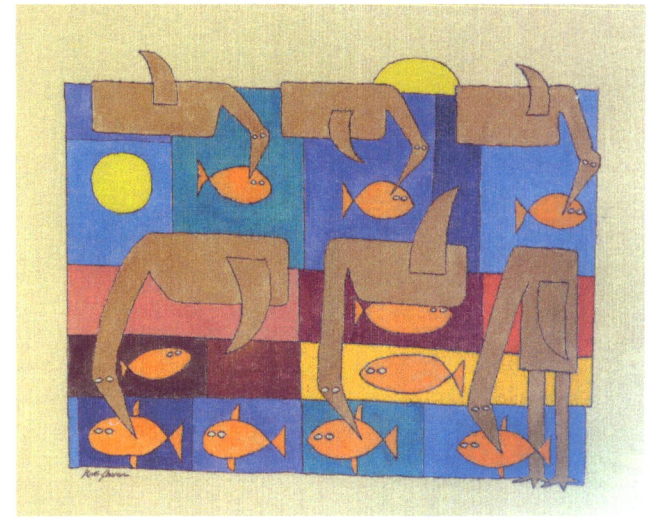

RS056

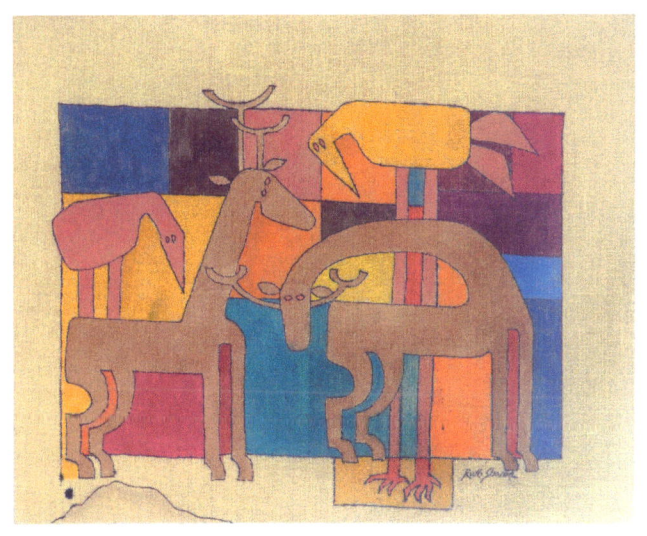

RS057

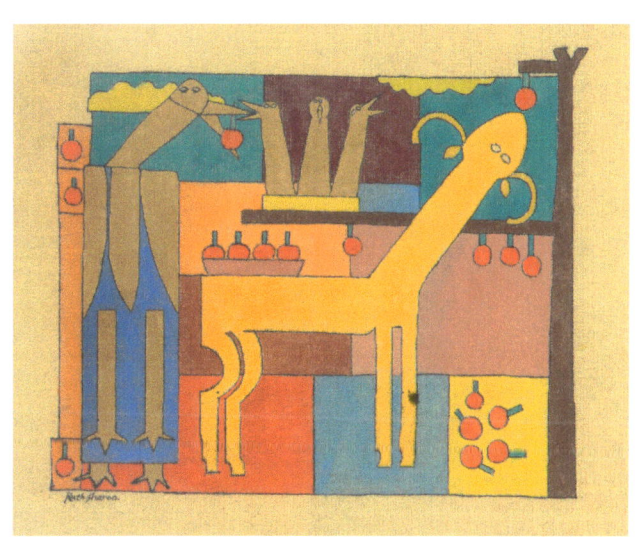

RS058

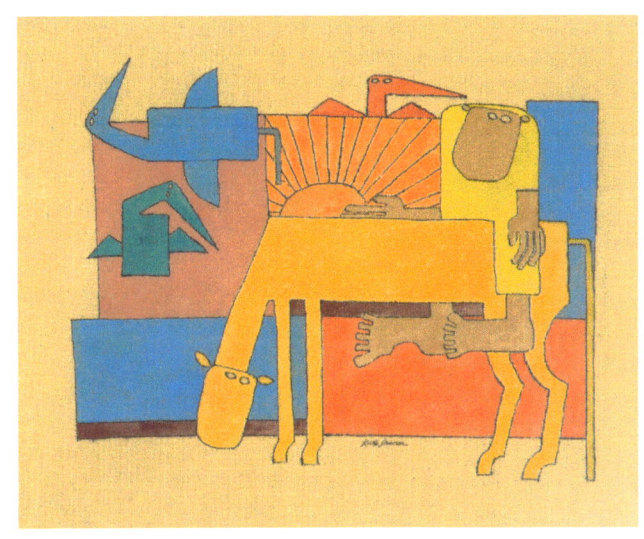

RS059

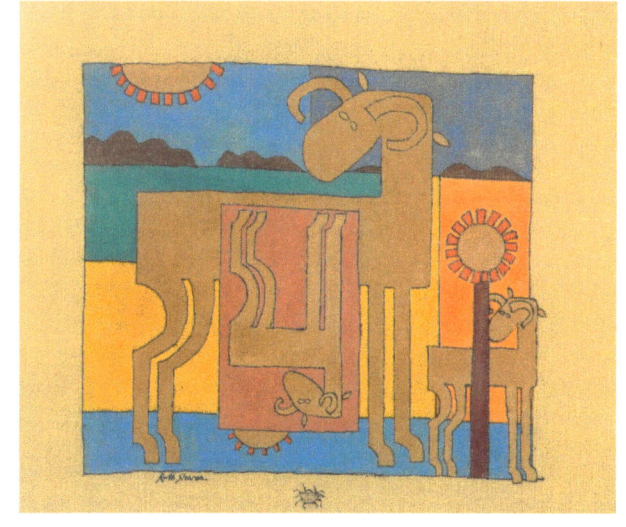

RS060

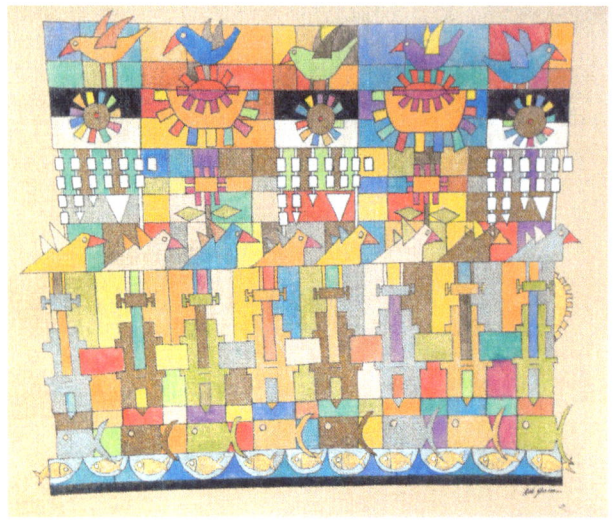

RS061

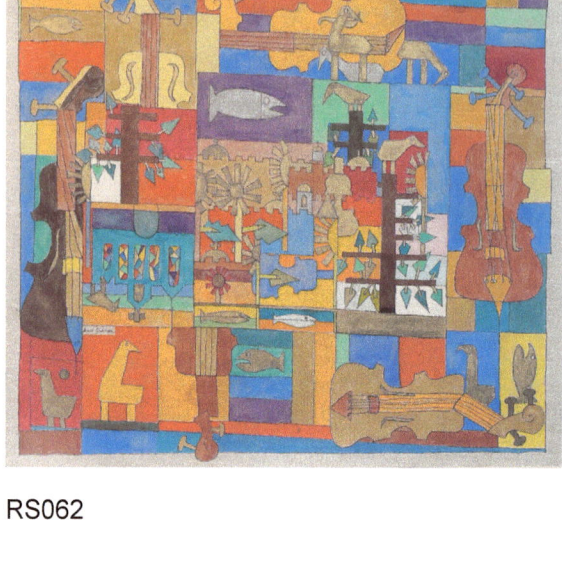

RS062

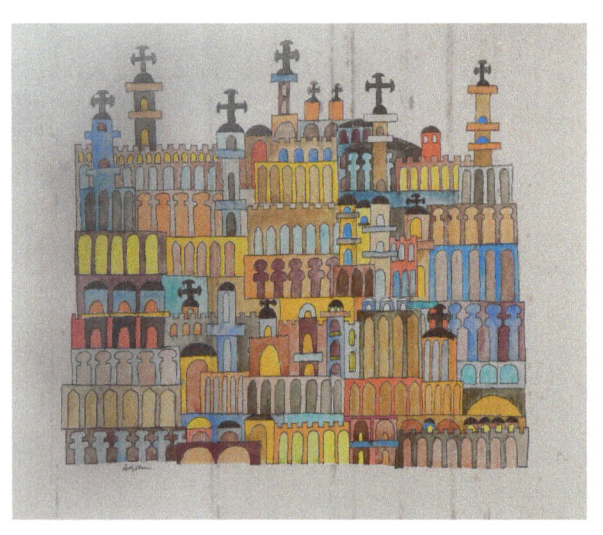

RS063

RS064

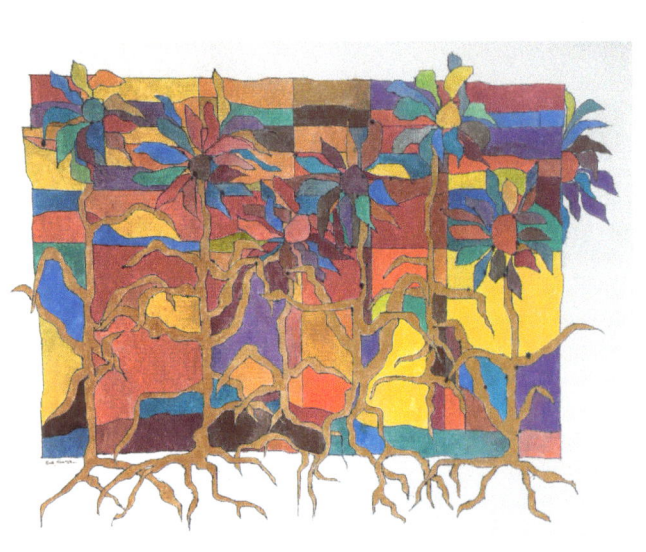

RS065

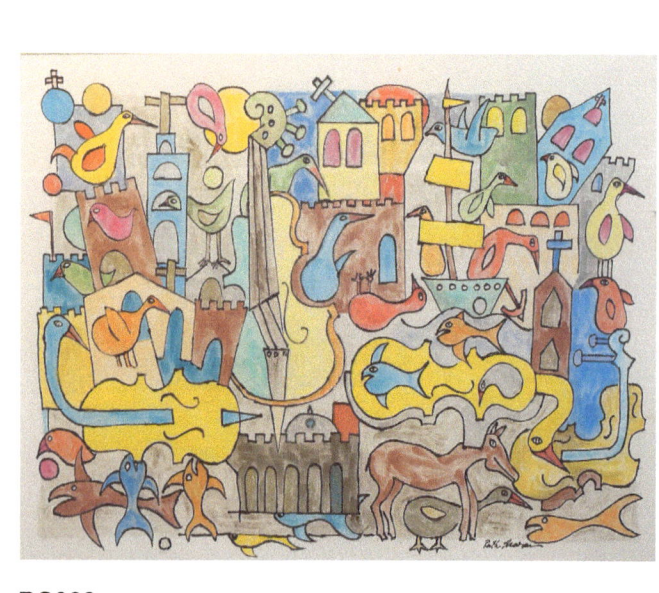

RS066

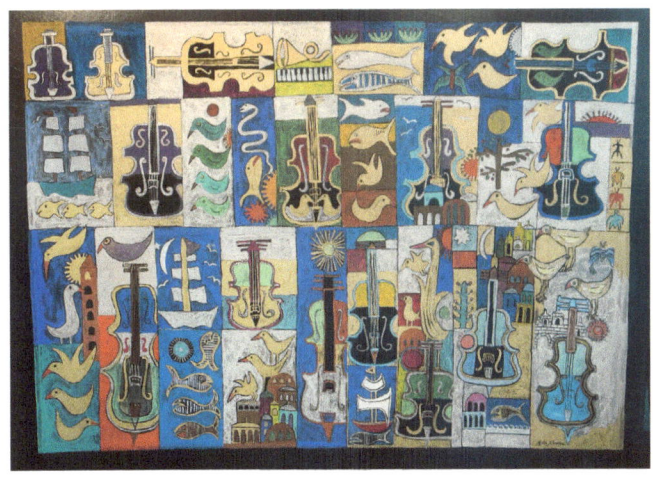

RS067

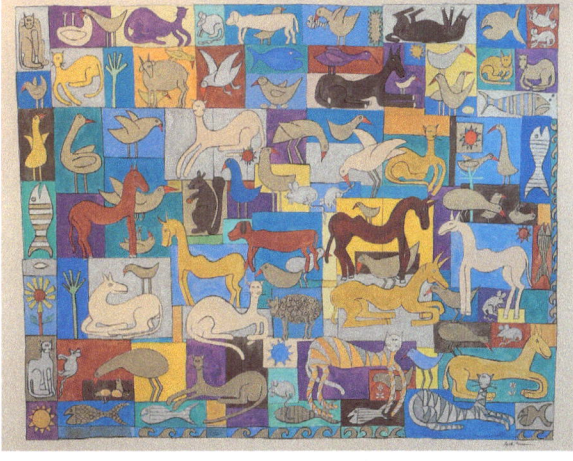

RS068

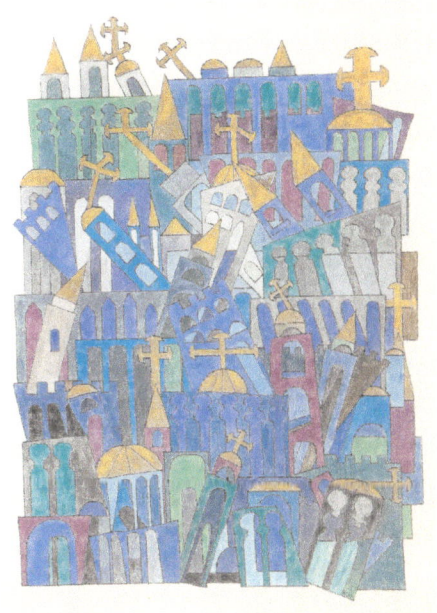

RS069

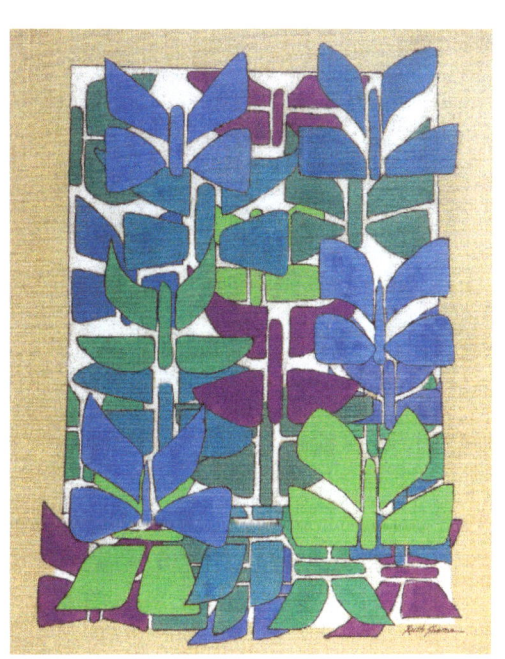

RS070

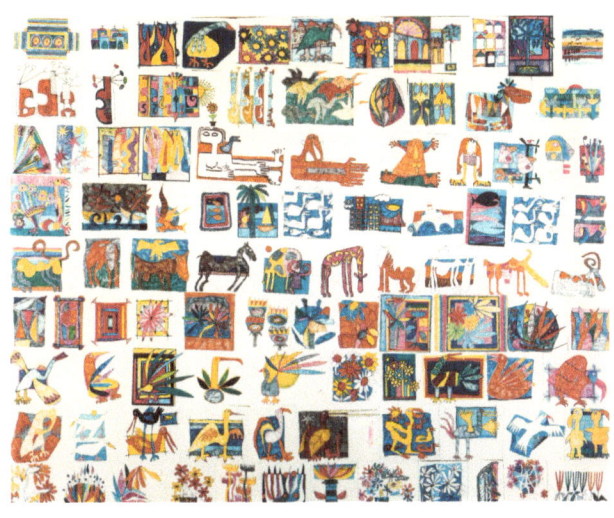

RS071

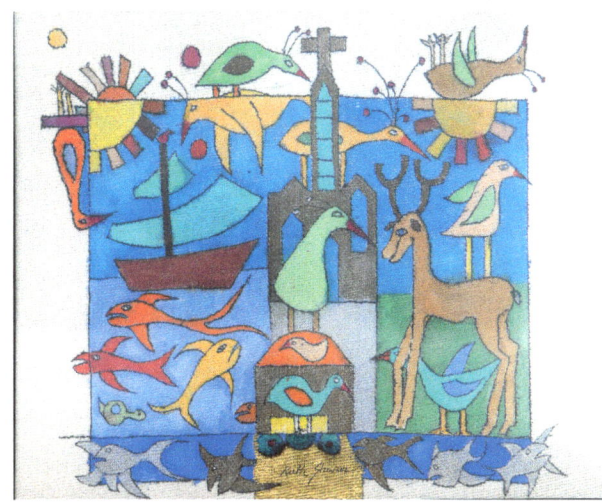

RS072

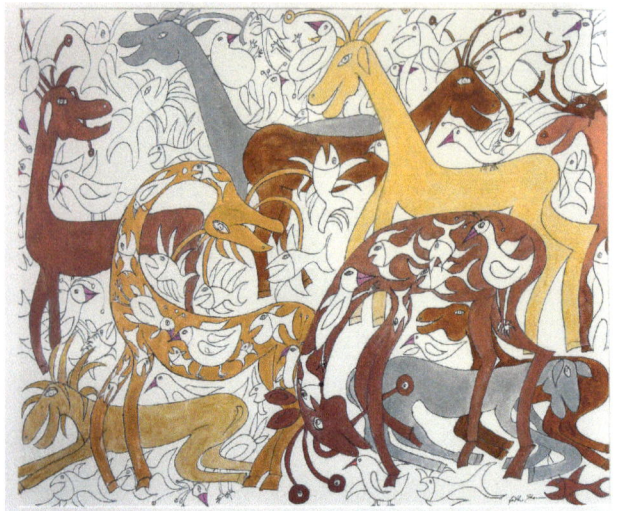

RS073

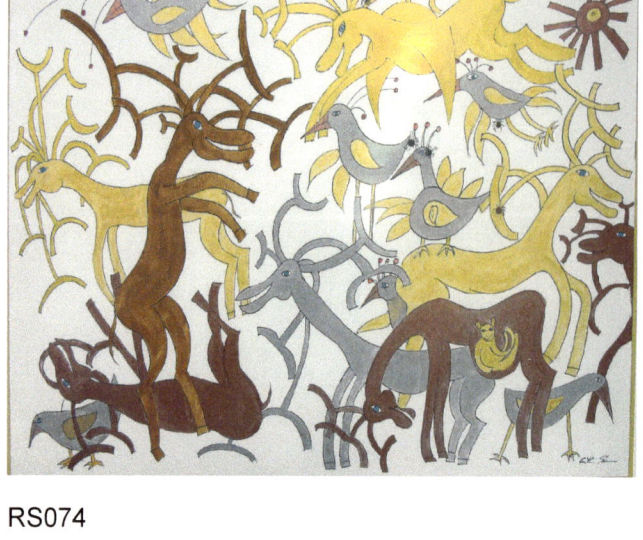

RS074

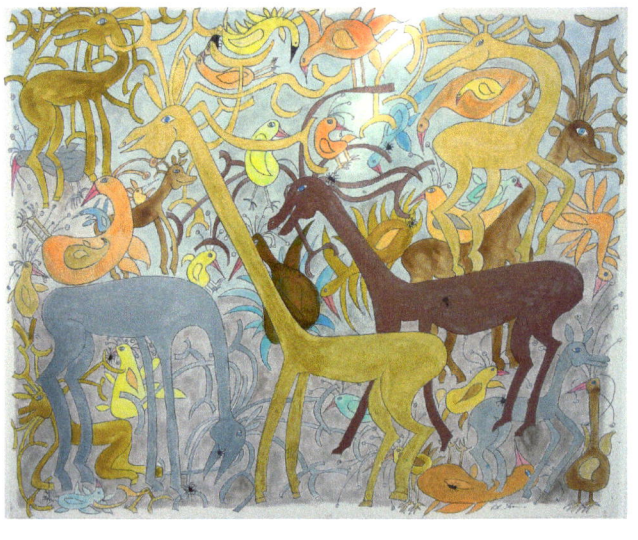

RS075

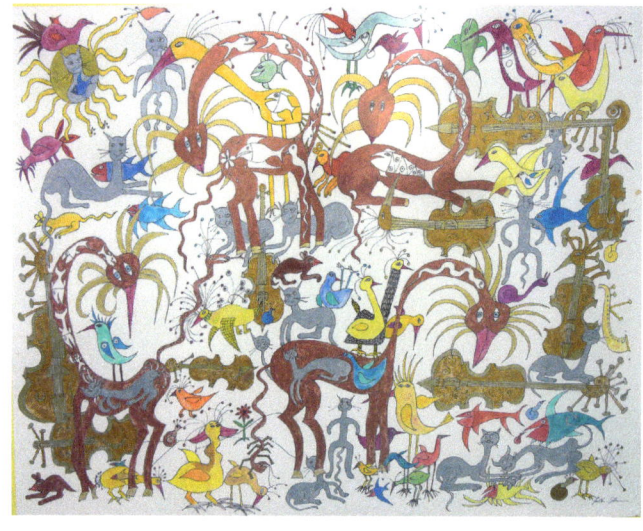

RS076

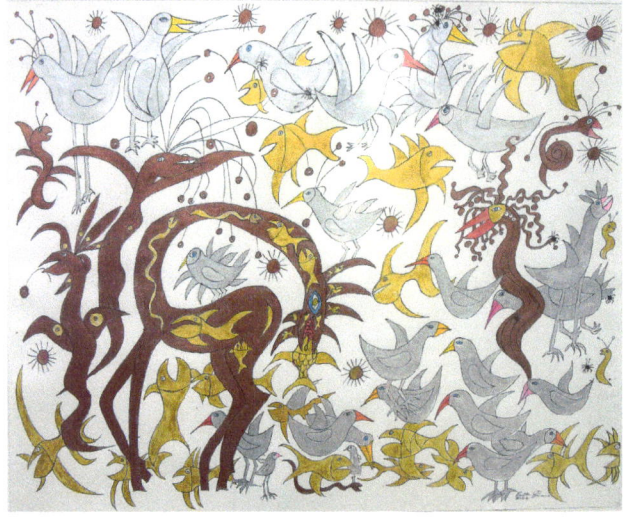

RS077

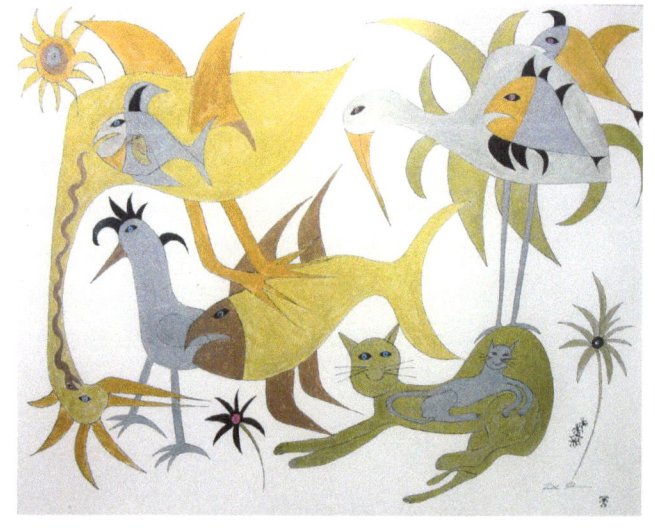

RS078

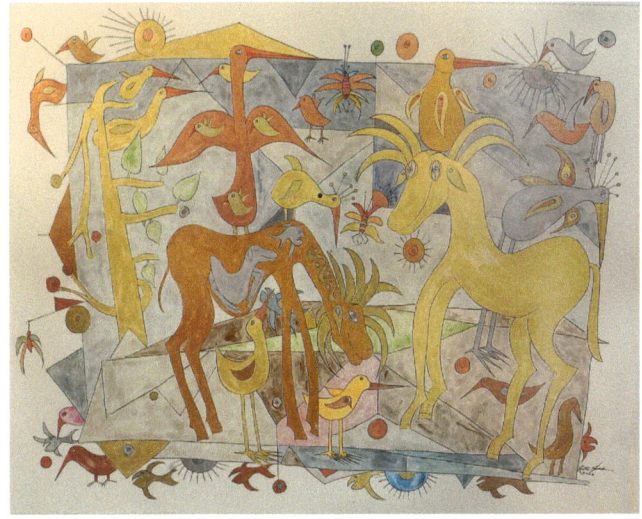

RS079

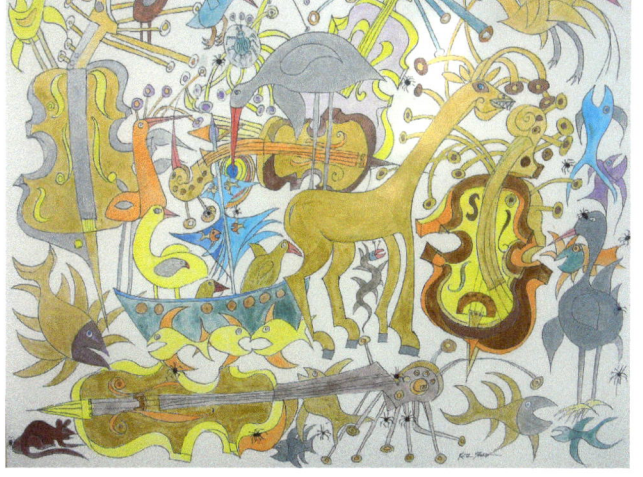

RS080

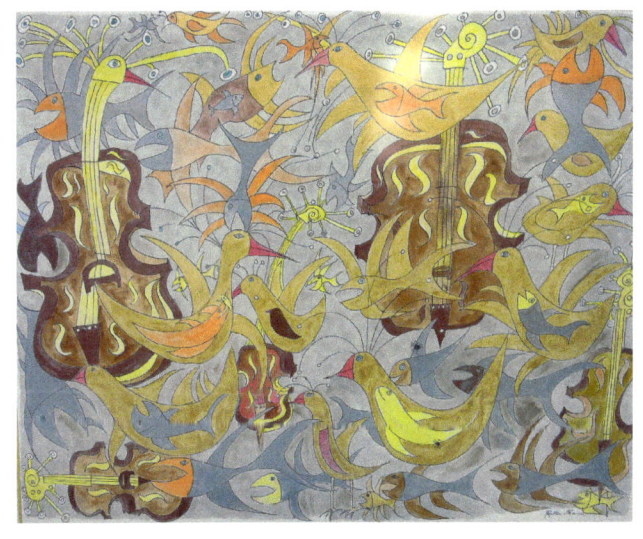

RS081

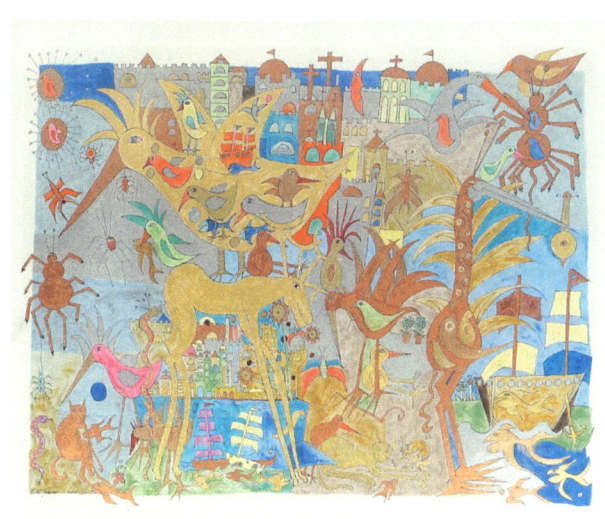

RS082

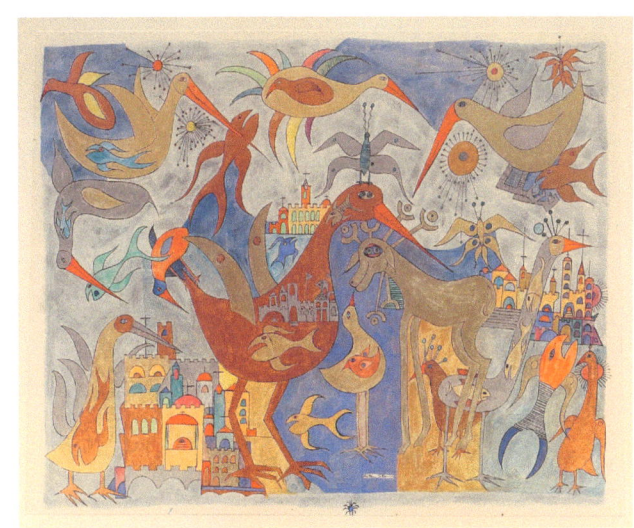

RS083

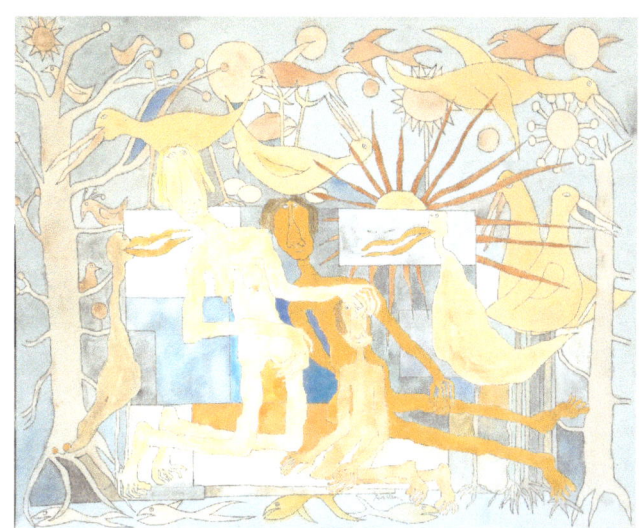

RS084

37

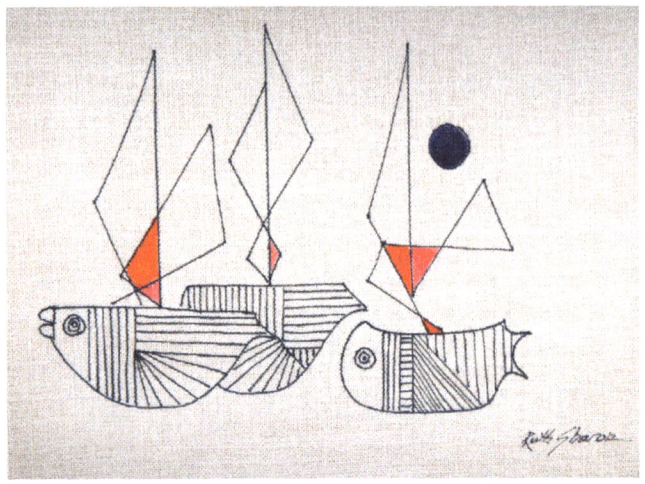

RS085

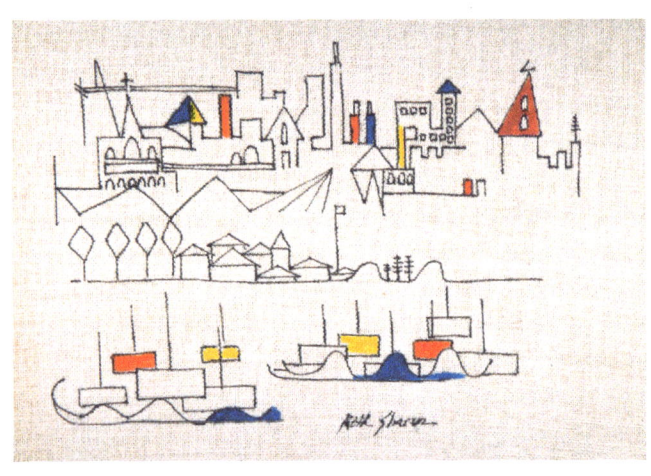

RS086

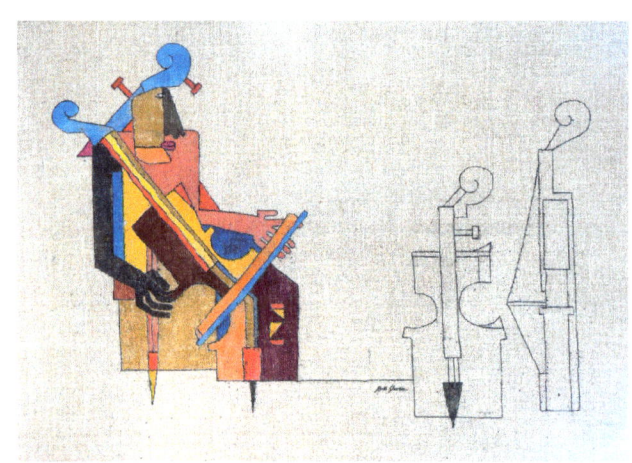

RS087

RS088

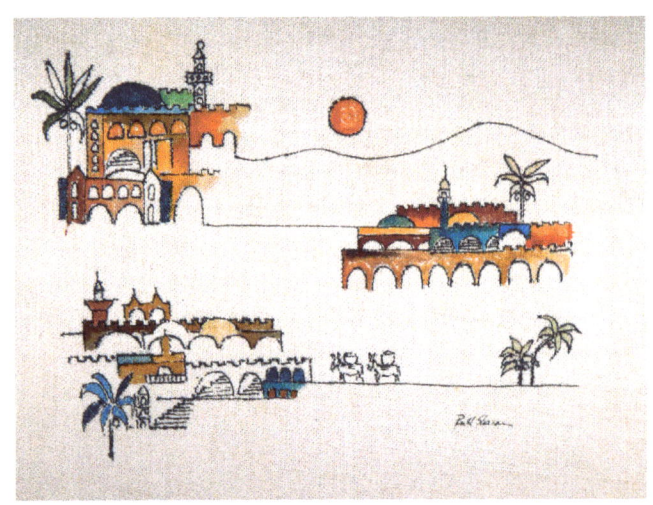

RS089

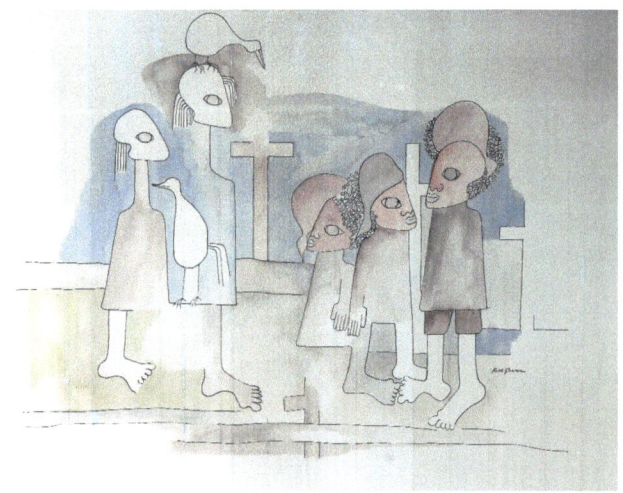

RS090

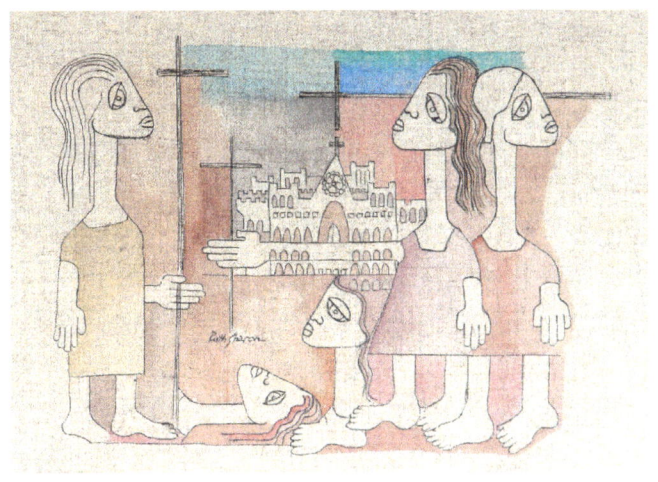

RS091

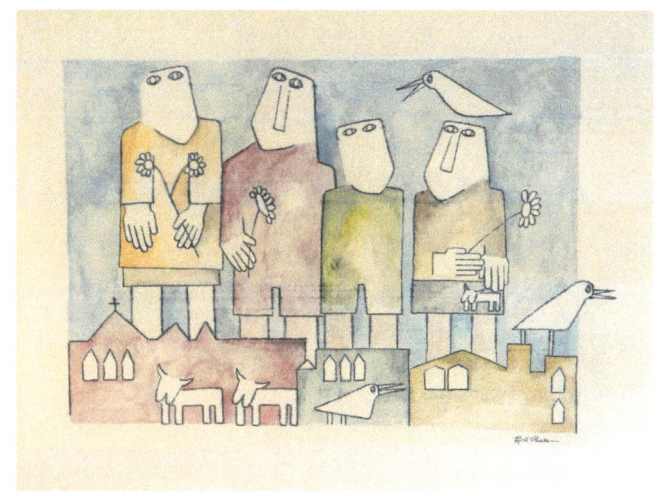

RS092

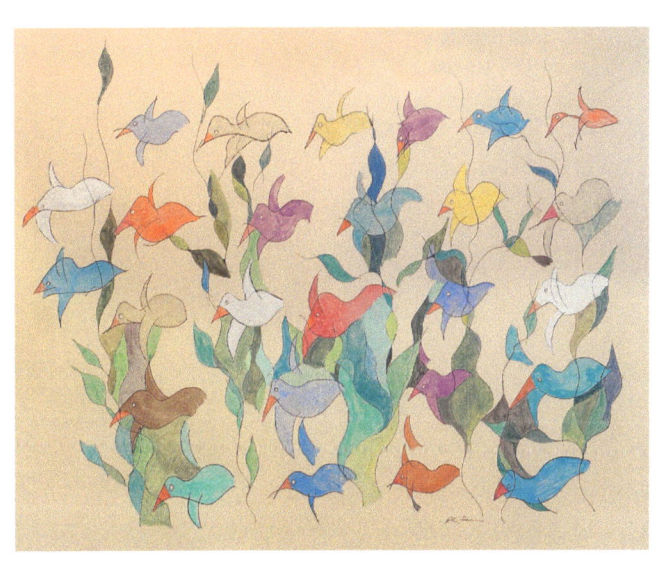

RS093

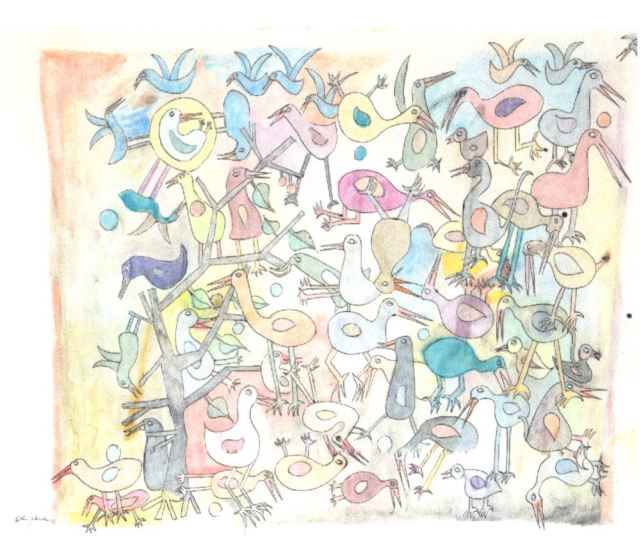

RS094

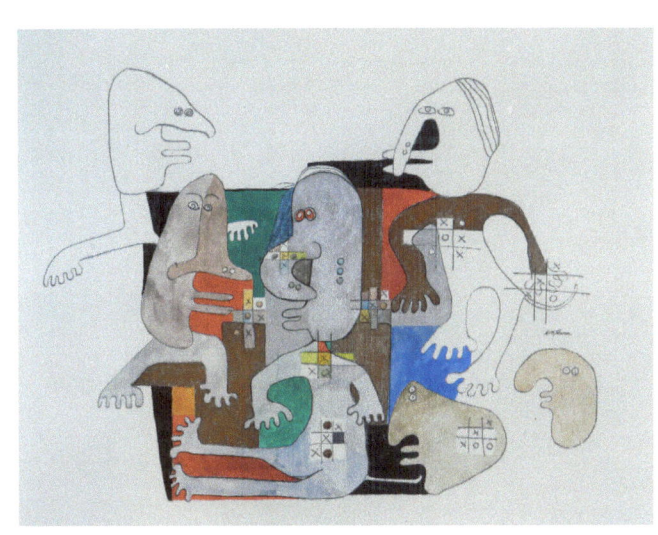

RS095

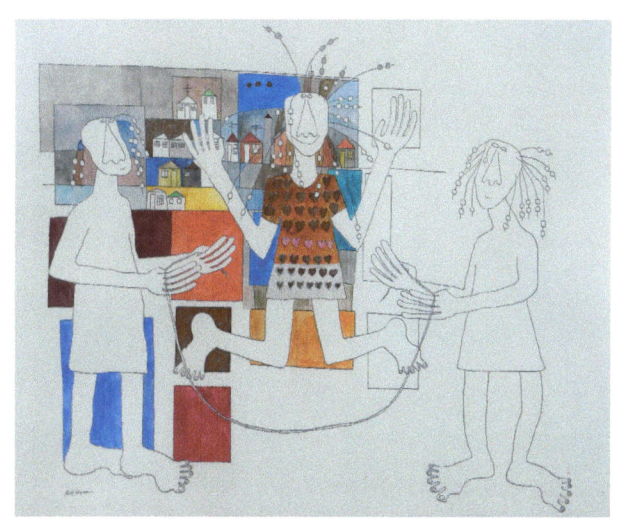

RS096

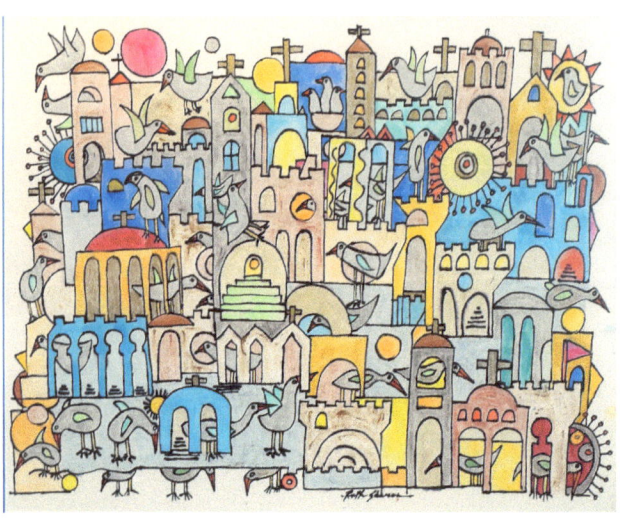
RS097

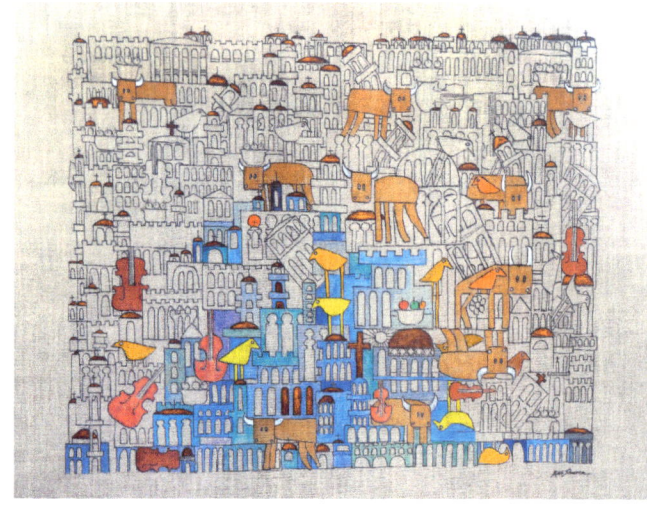
RS098

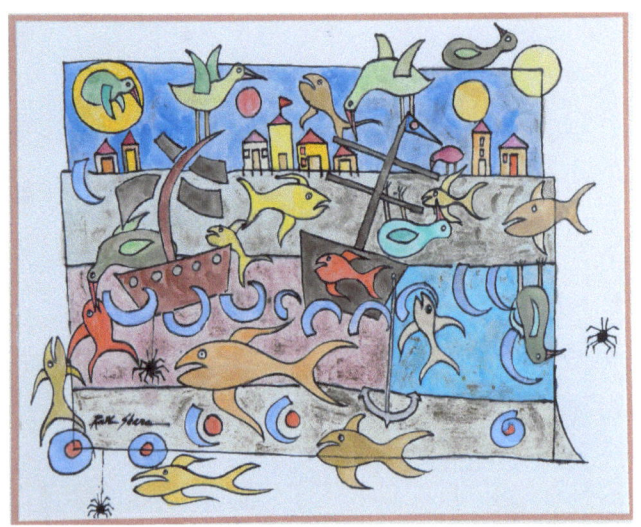
RS099

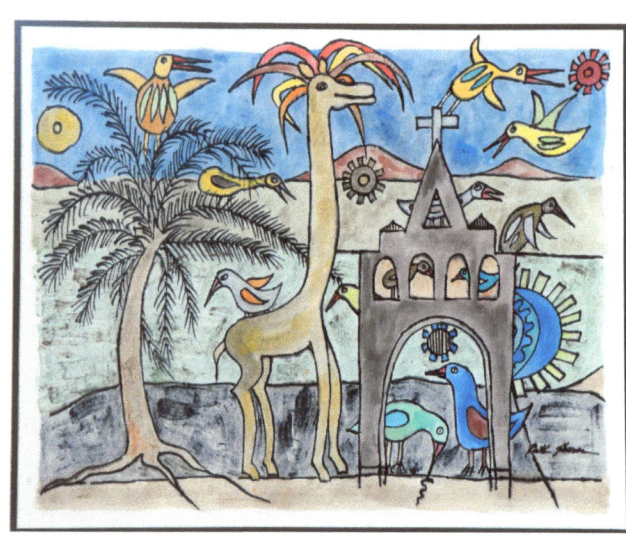
RS100

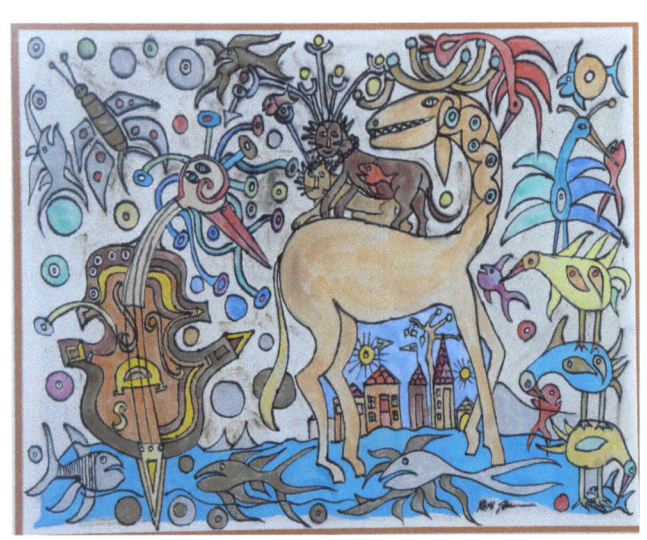
RS101

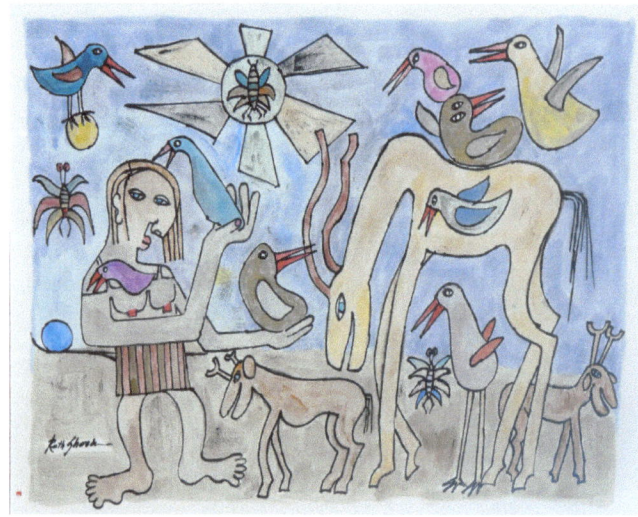
RS102

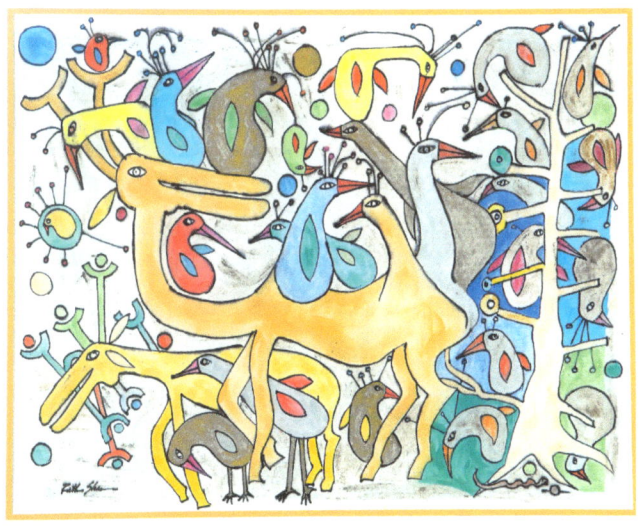

RS103

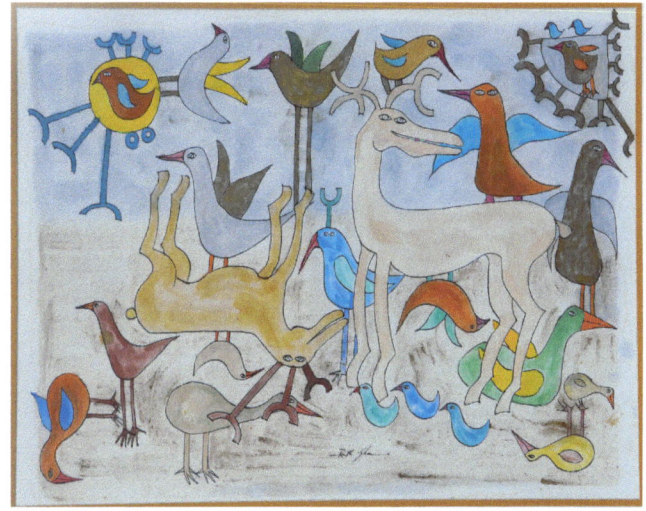

RS104

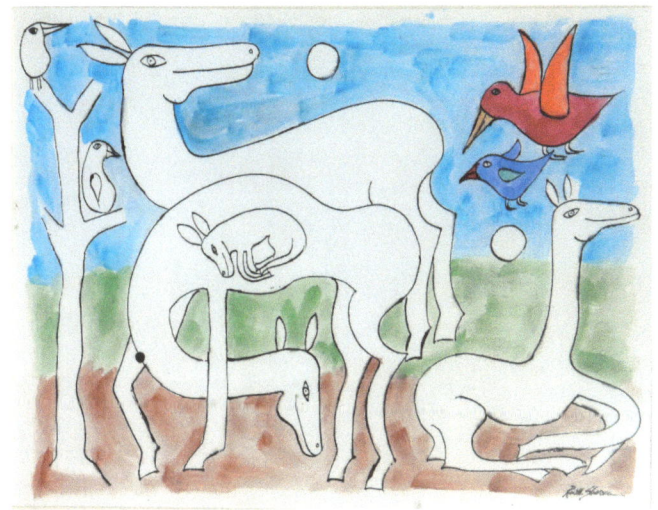

RS105

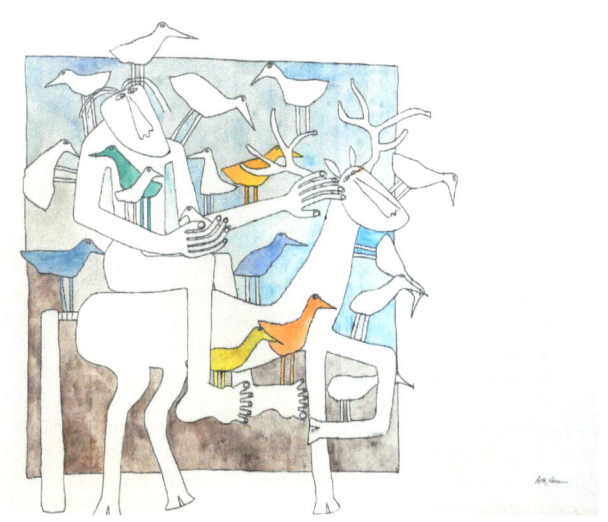

RS106

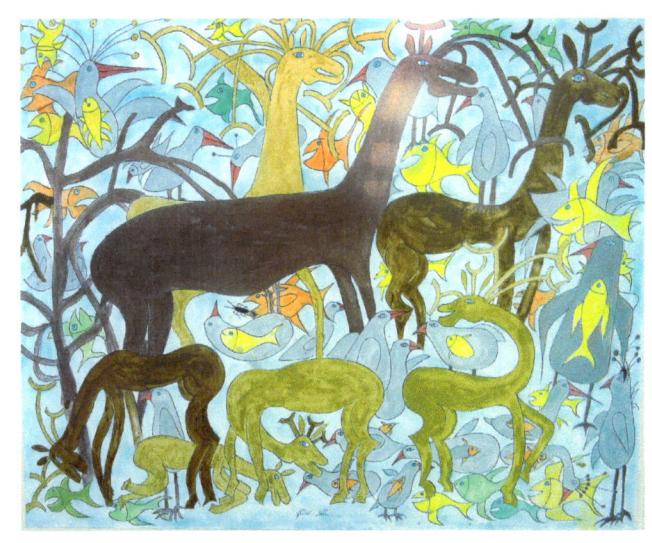

RS107

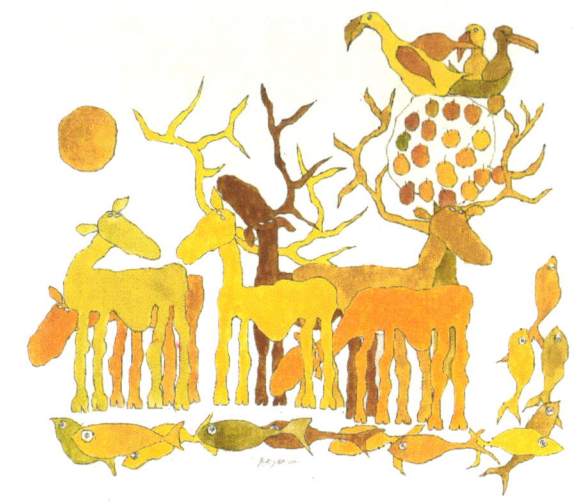

RS108

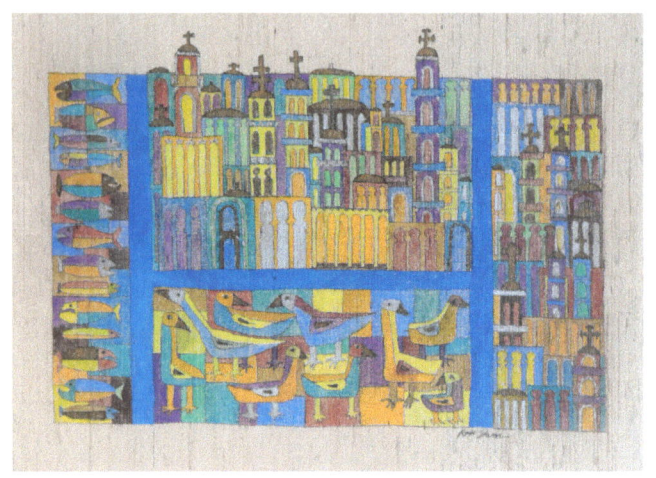
RS109

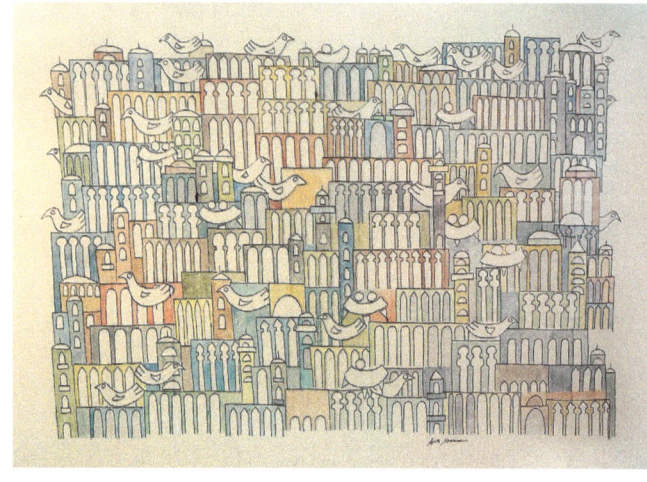
RS110

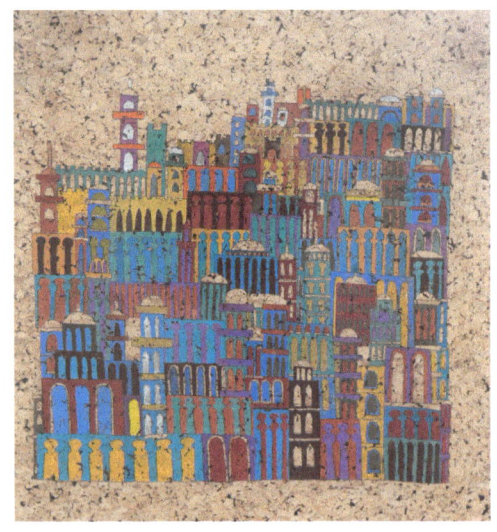
RS111

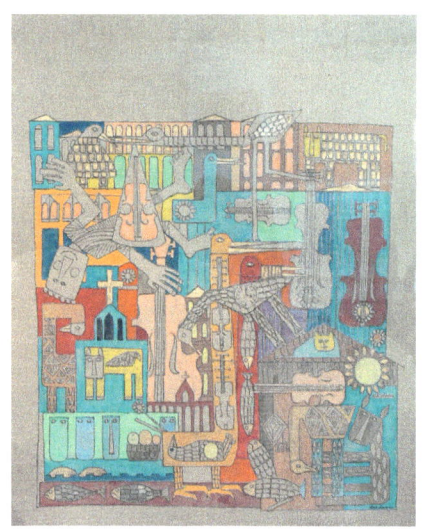
RS112

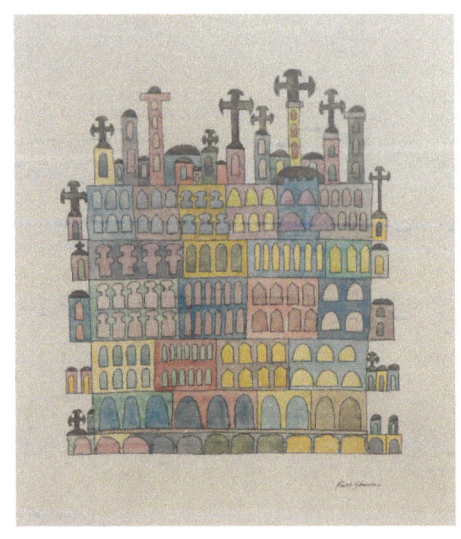
RS113

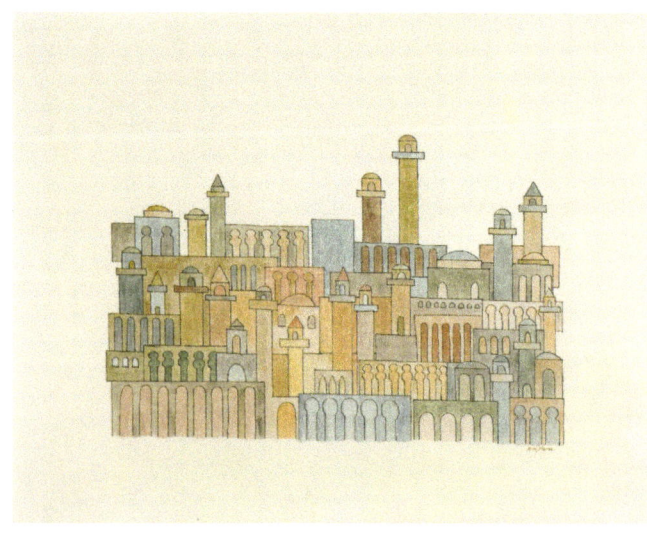
RS114

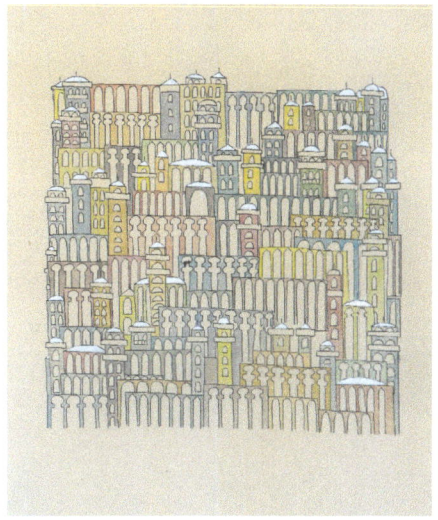

RS115

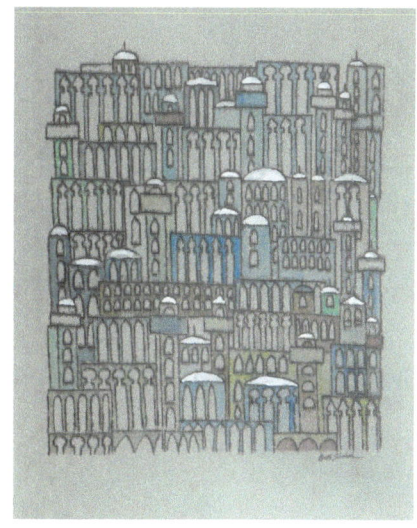

RS116

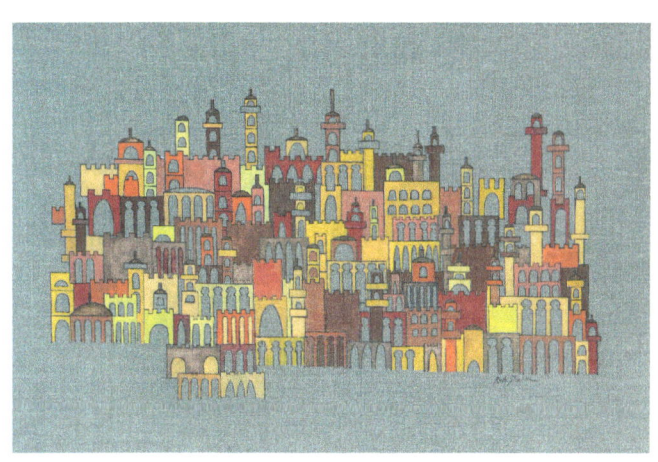

RS117

RS118

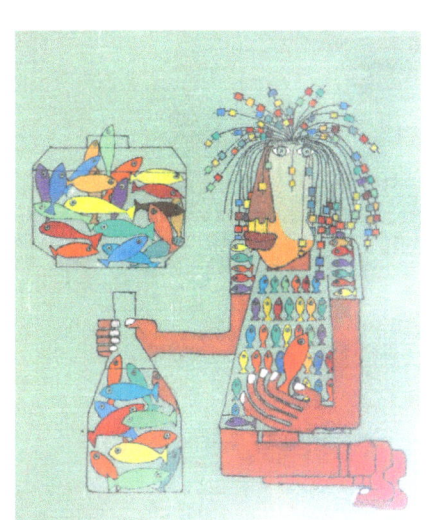

RS119

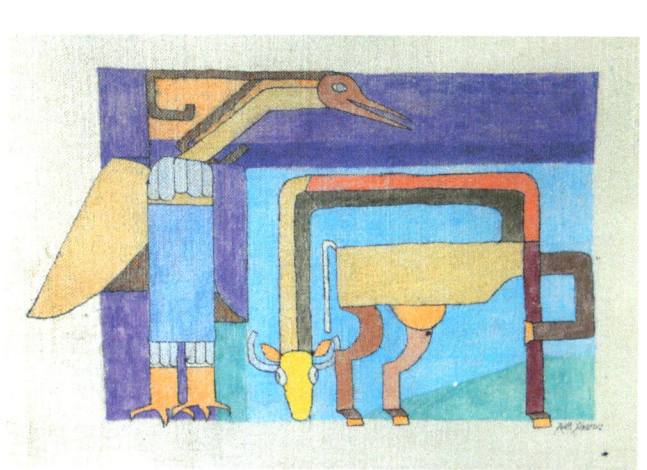

RS120

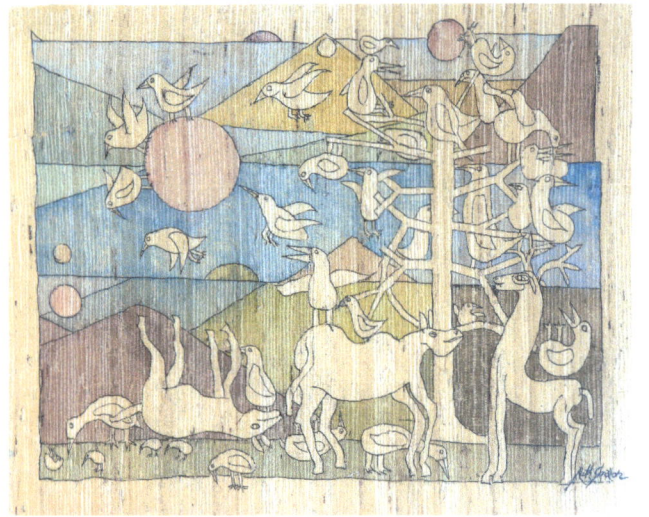

RS121

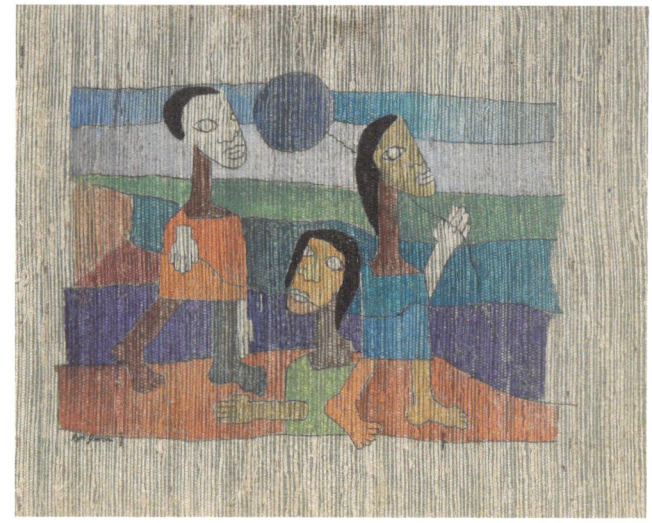

RS122

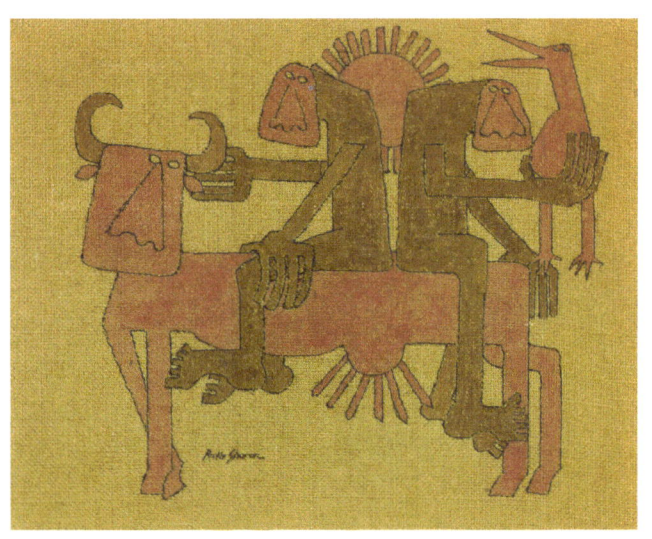

RS123

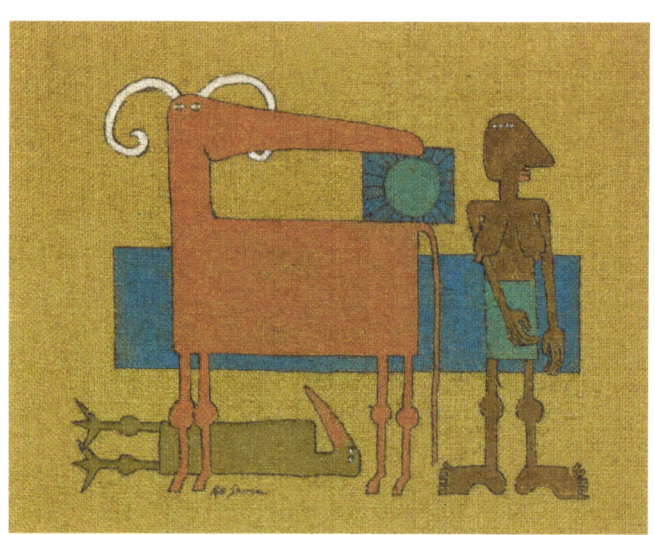

RS124

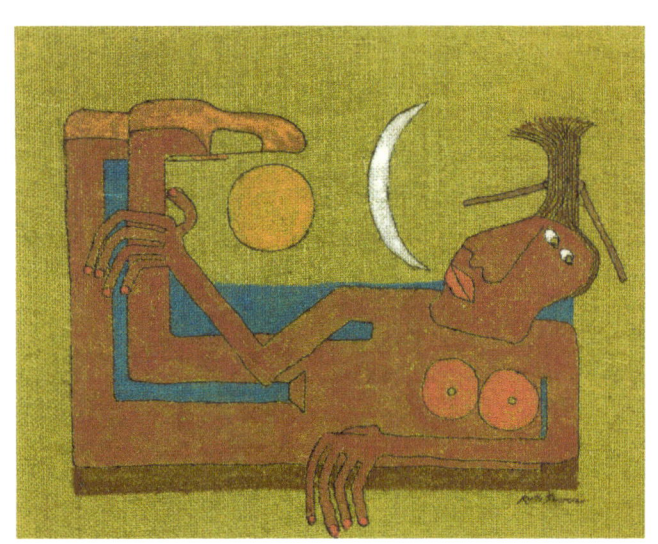

RS125

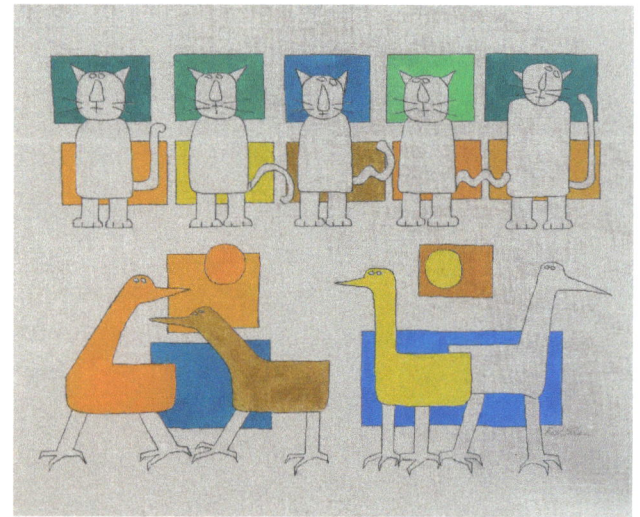

RS126

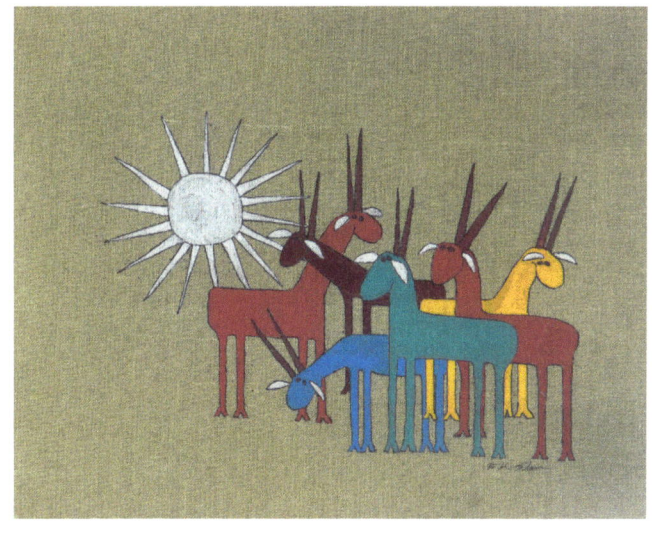

RS127

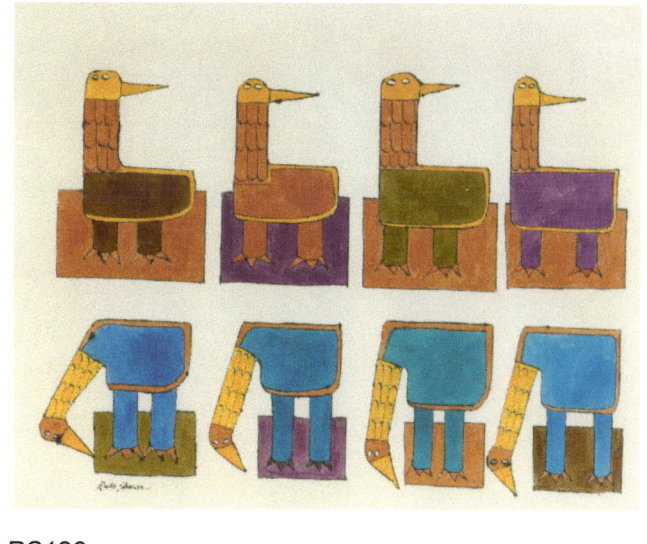

RS128

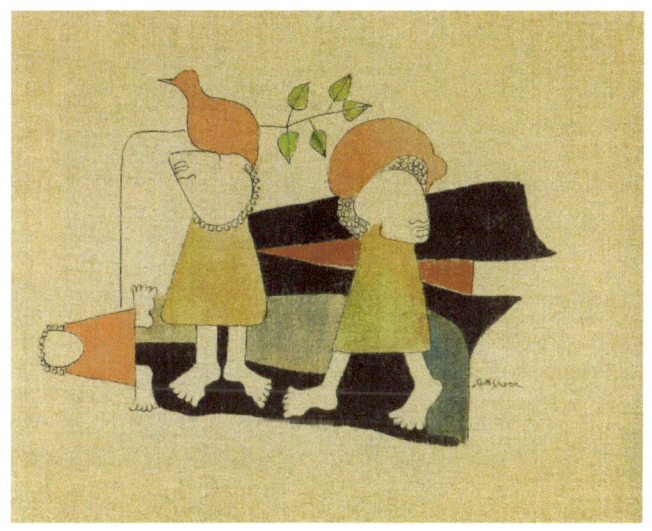

RS129

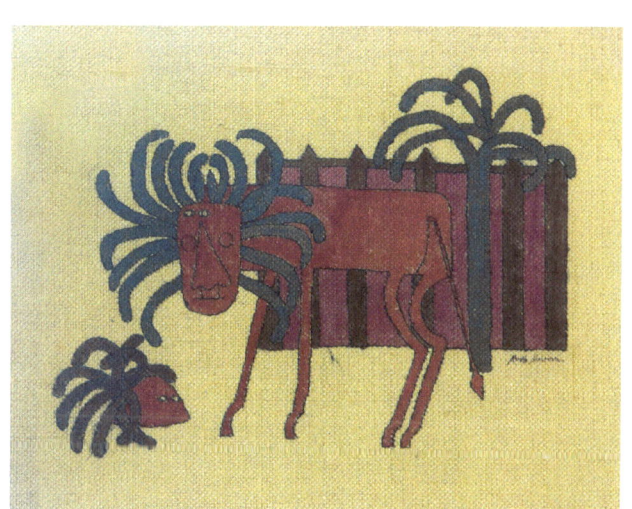

RS130

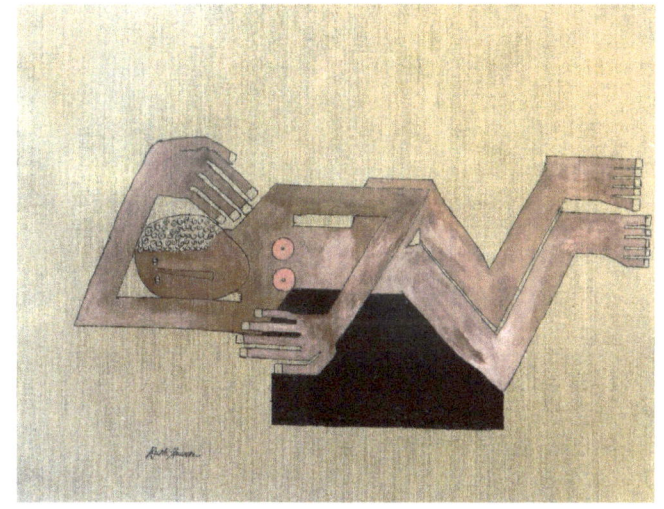

RS131

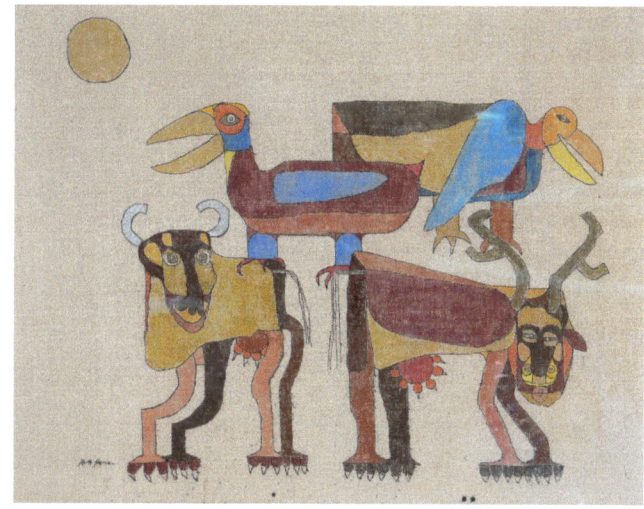

RS132

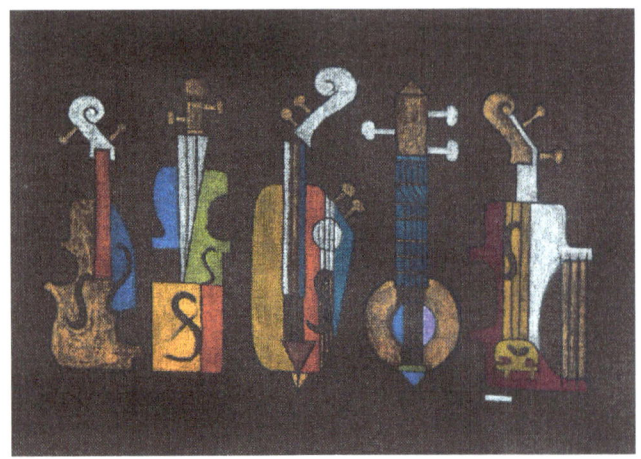

RS133

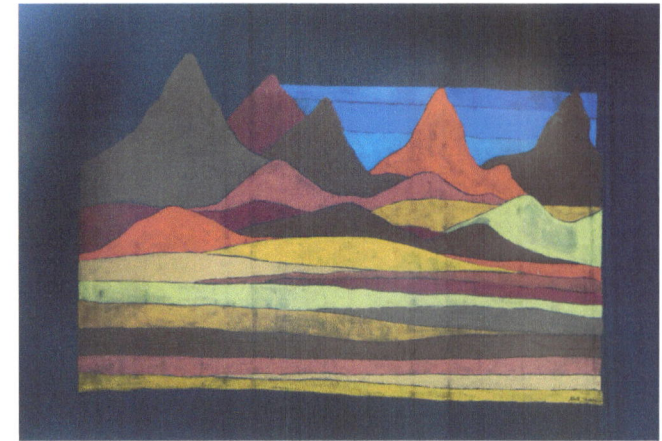

RS134

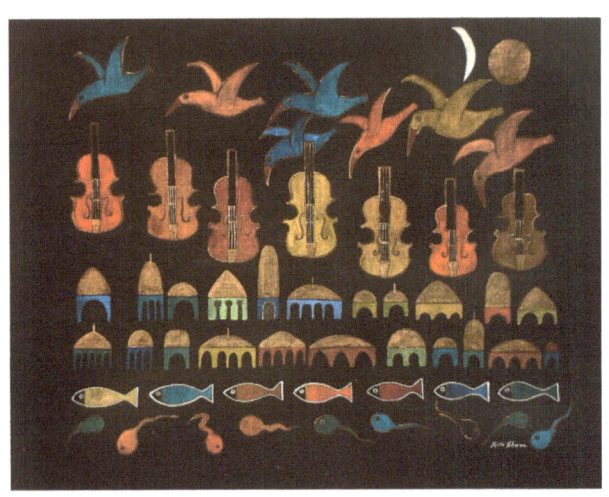

RS135

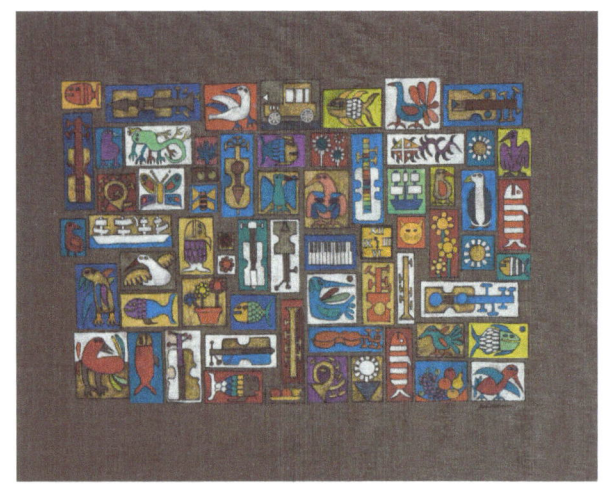

RS136

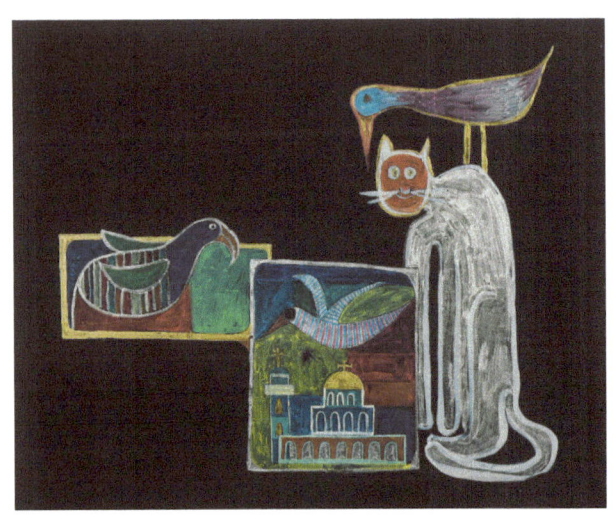

RS137

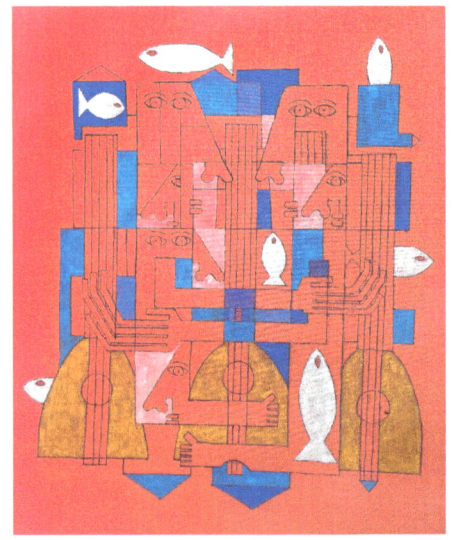

RS138

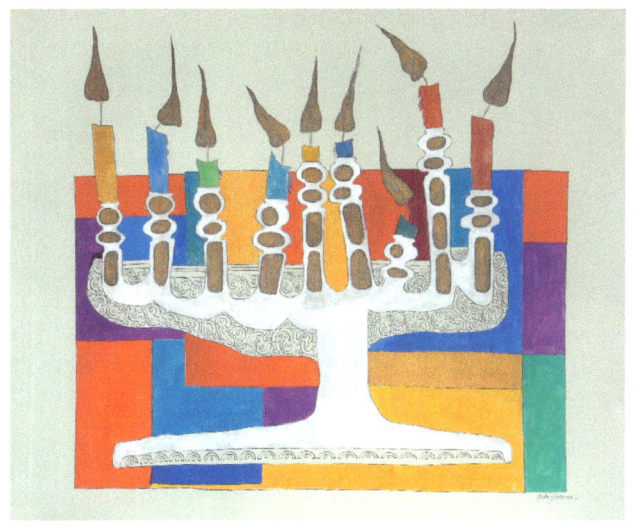
RS139

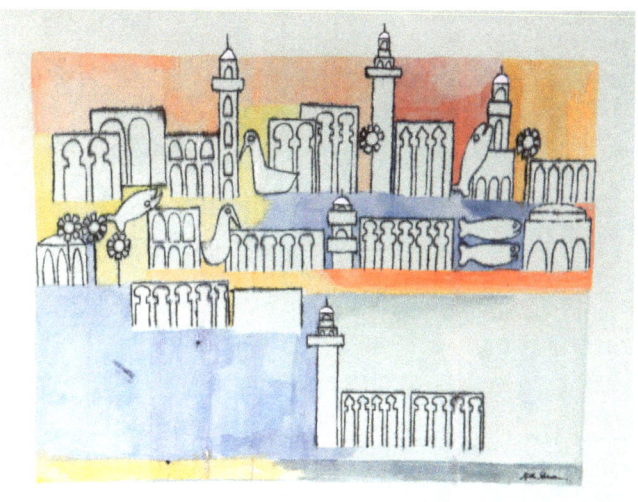
RS140

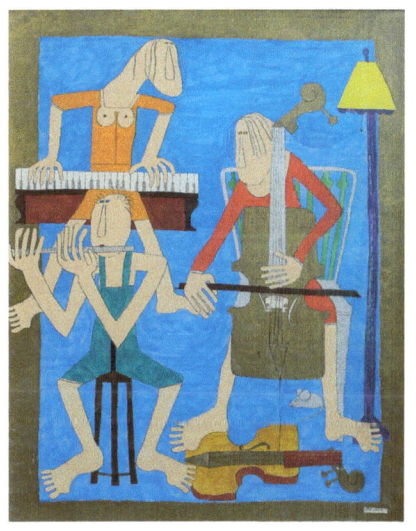
RS141

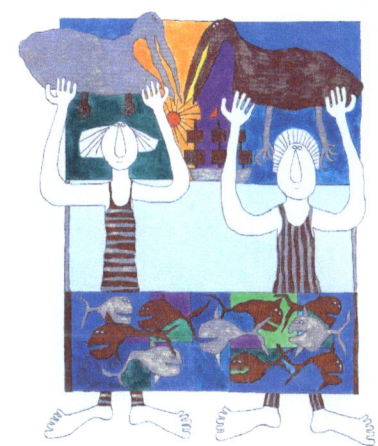
RS142

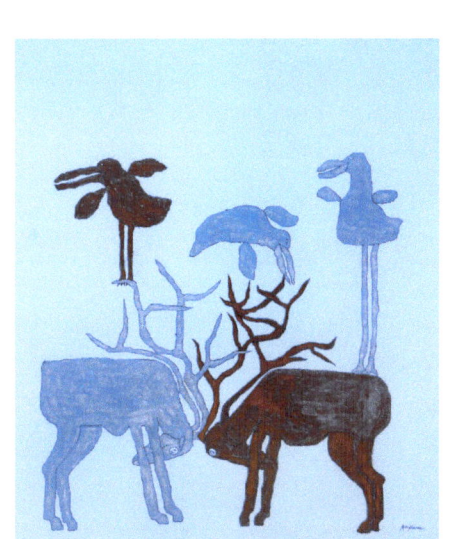
RS143

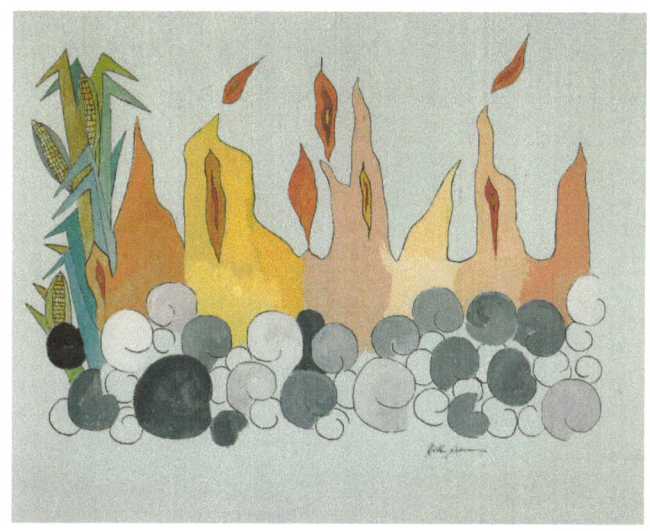
RS144

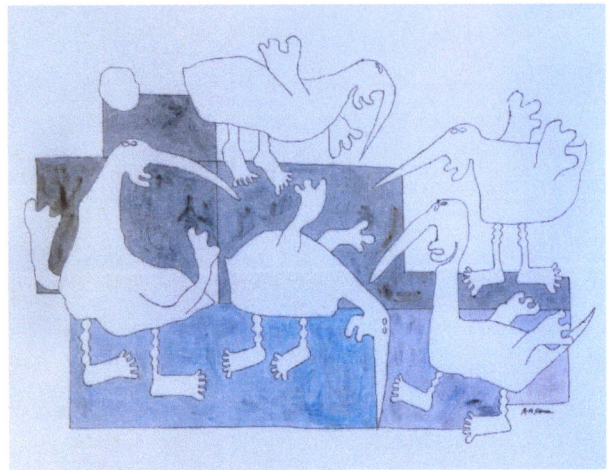

RS145

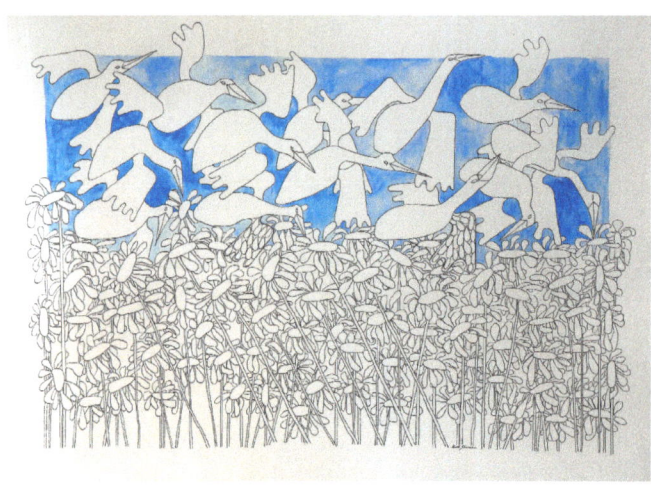

RS146

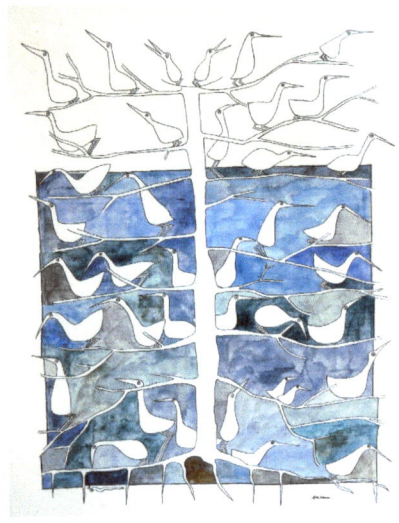

RS147

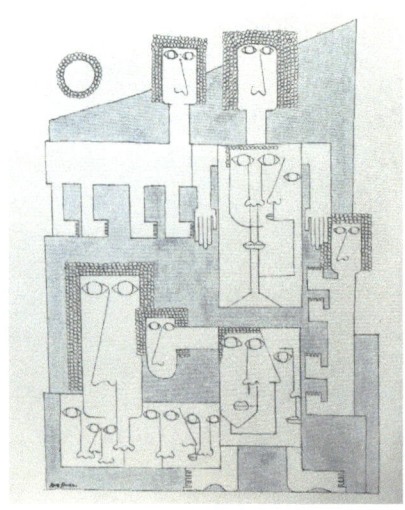

RS148

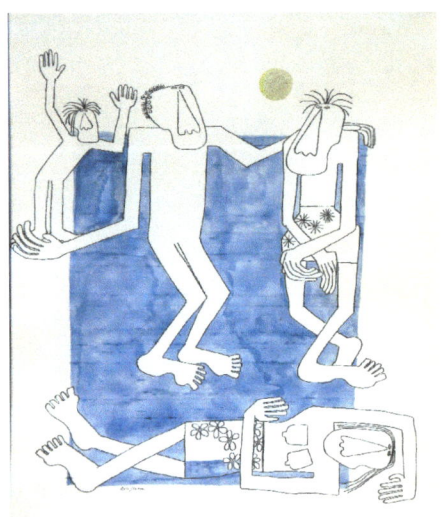

RS149

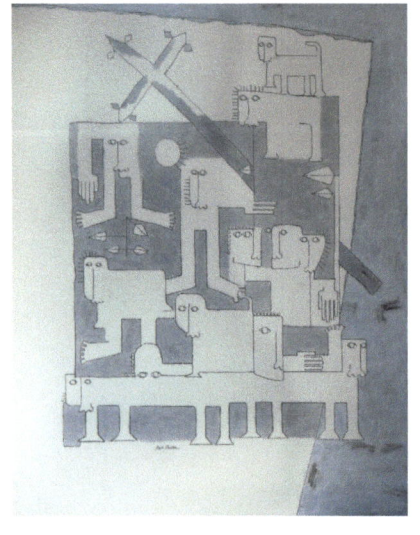

RS150

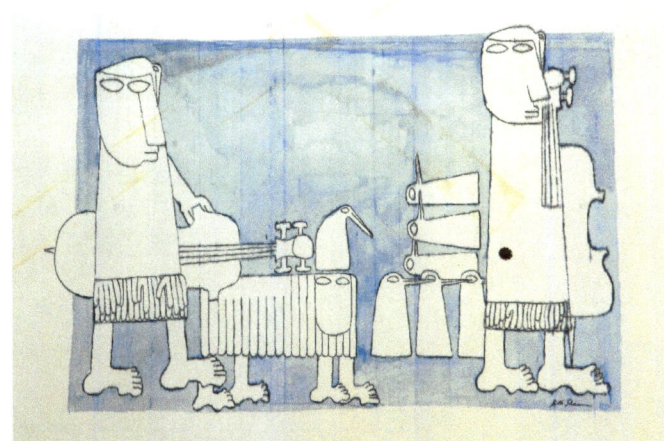

RS151

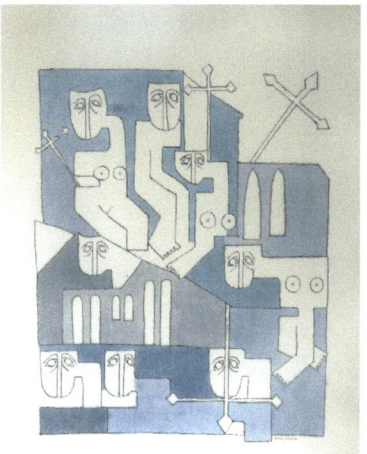

RS152

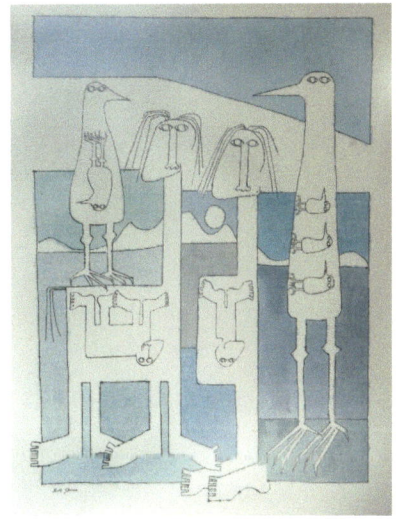

RS153

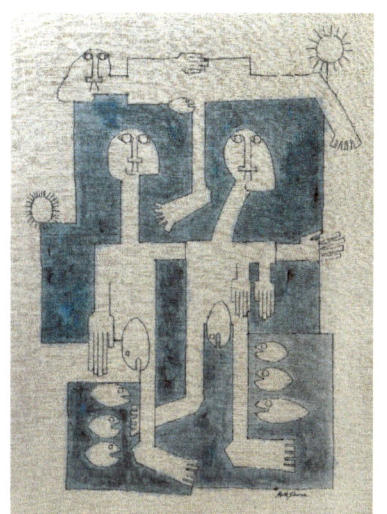

RS154

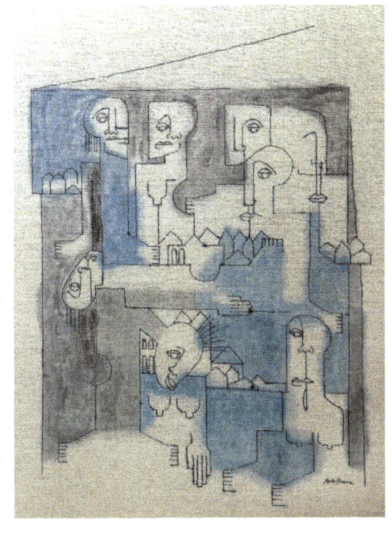

RS155

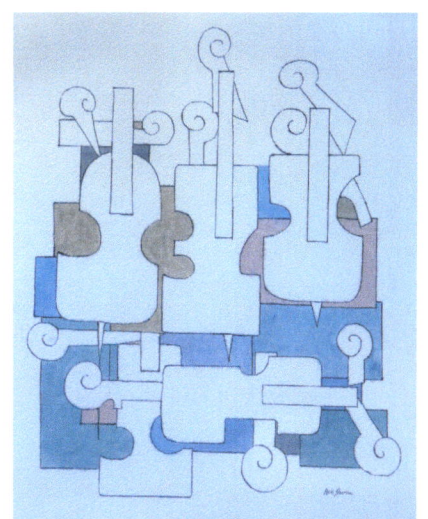

RS156

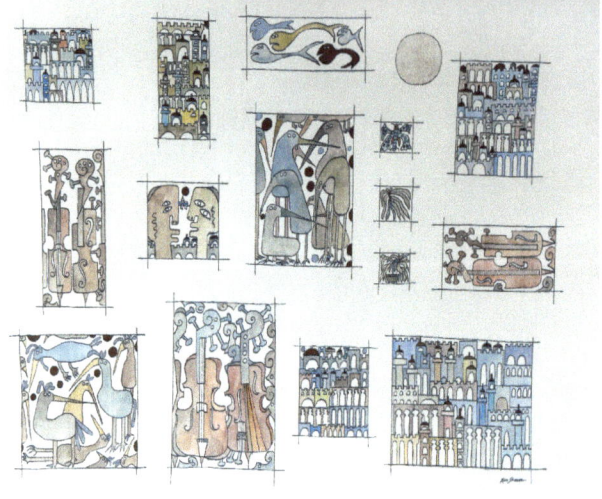

RS157

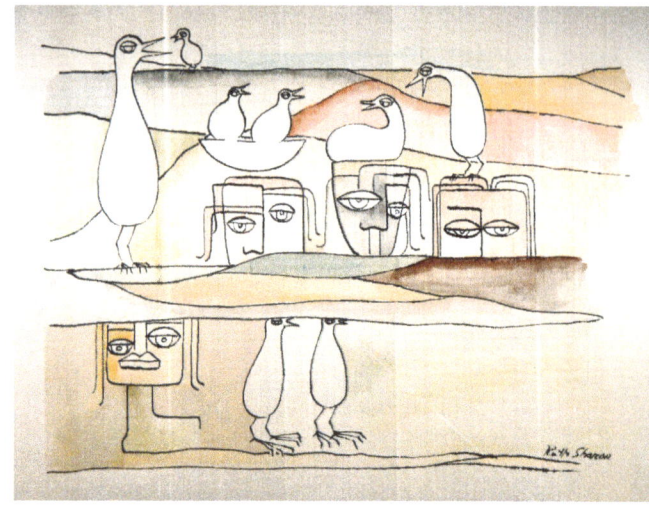

RS158

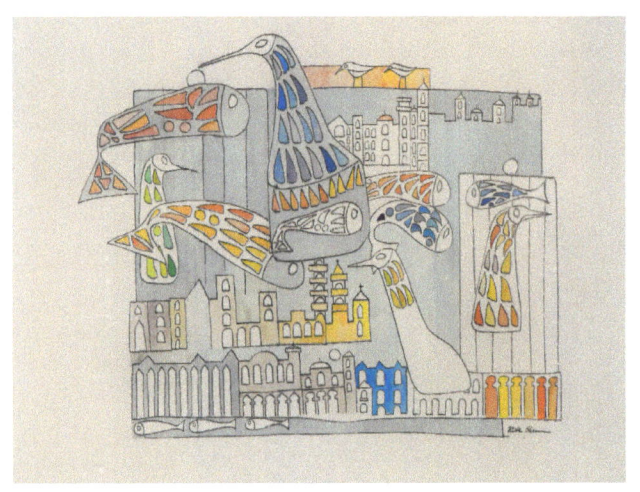

RS159

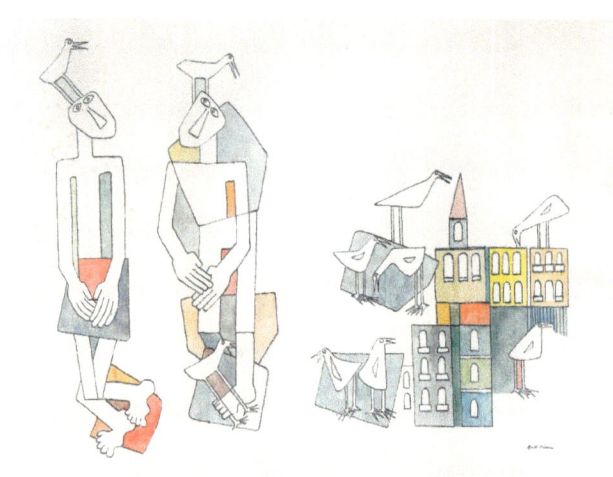

RS160

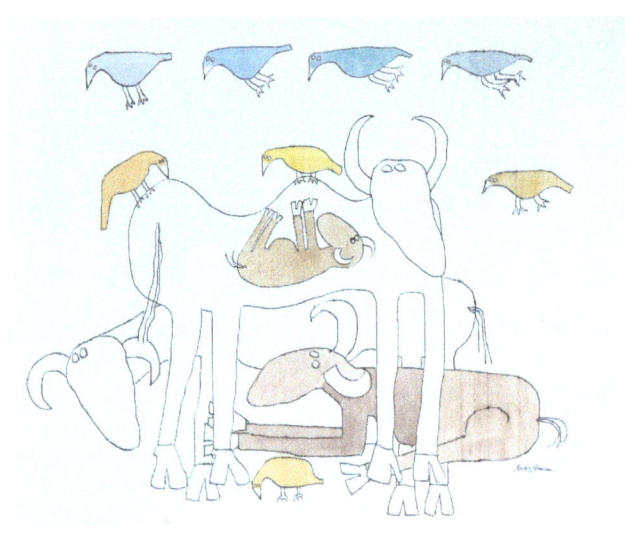

RS161

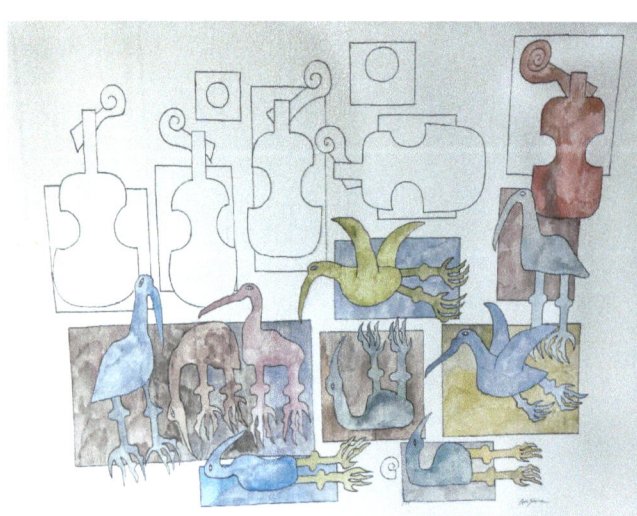

RS162

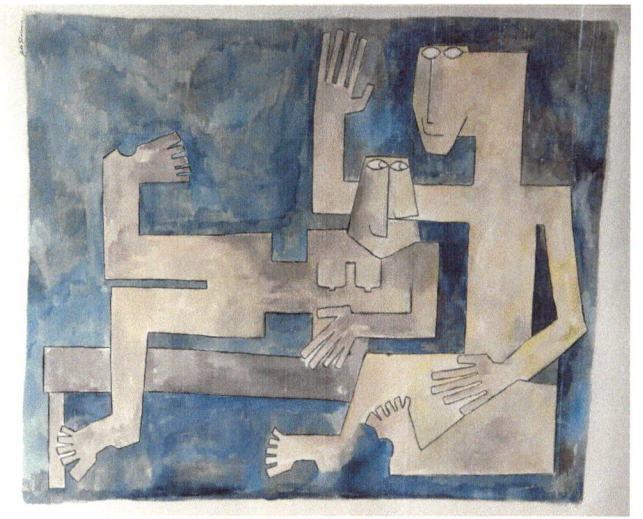

RS163

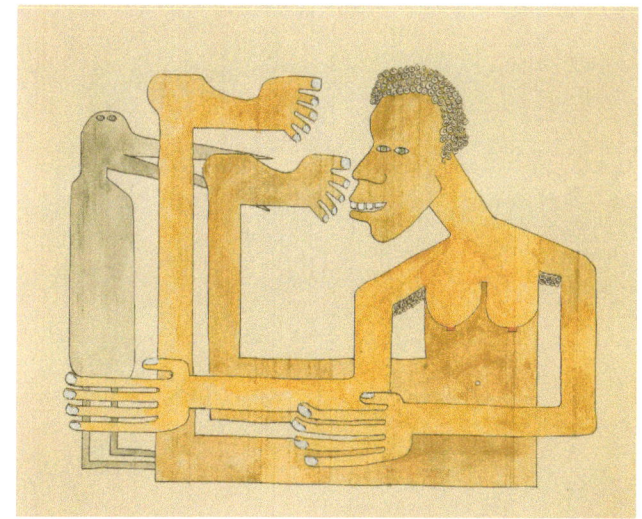

RS164

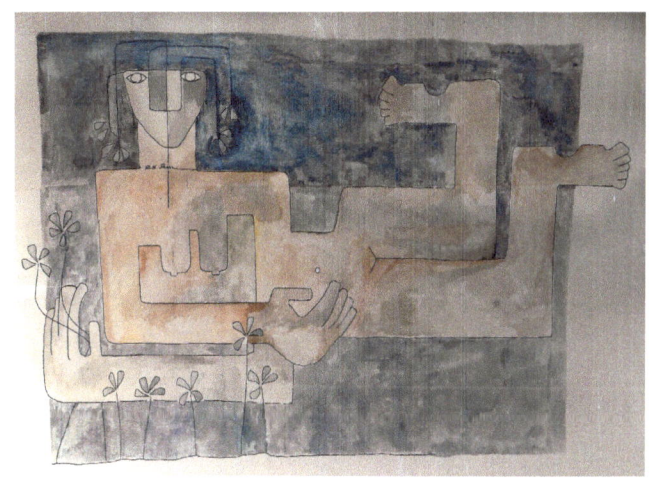

RS165

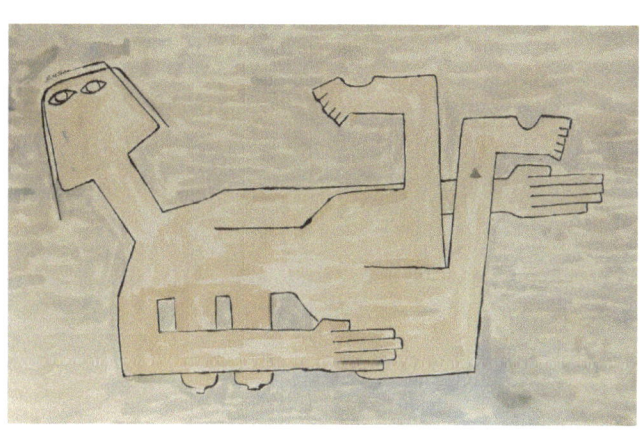

RS166

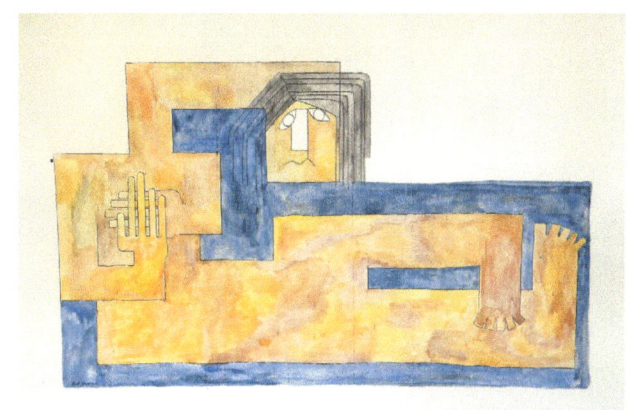

RS167

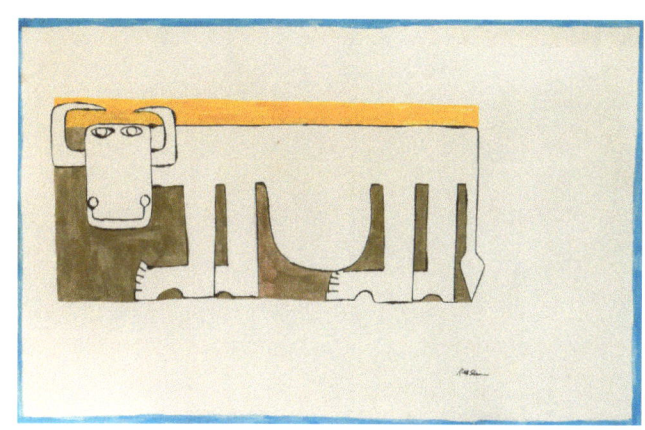

RS168

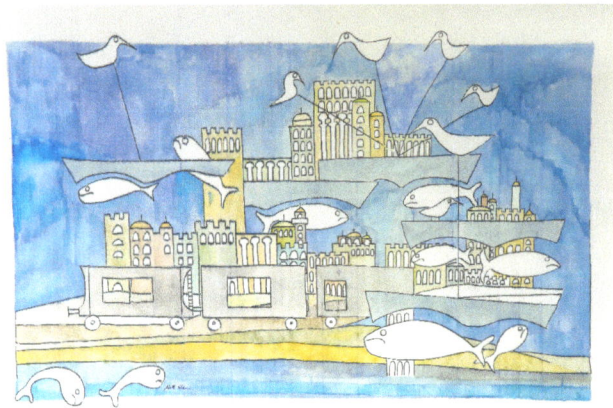
RS169

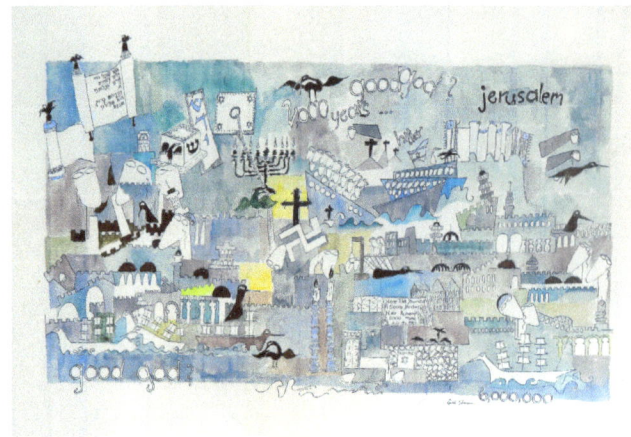
RS170

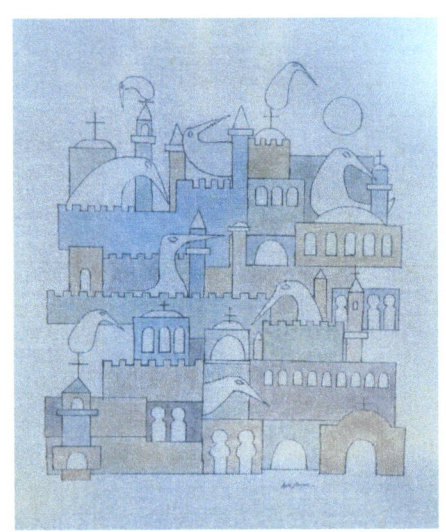
RS171

RS172

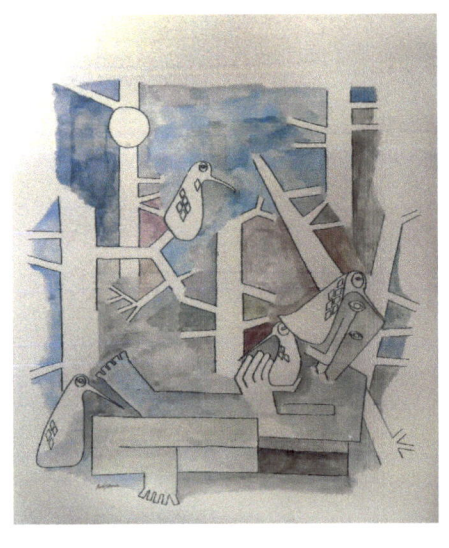
RS173

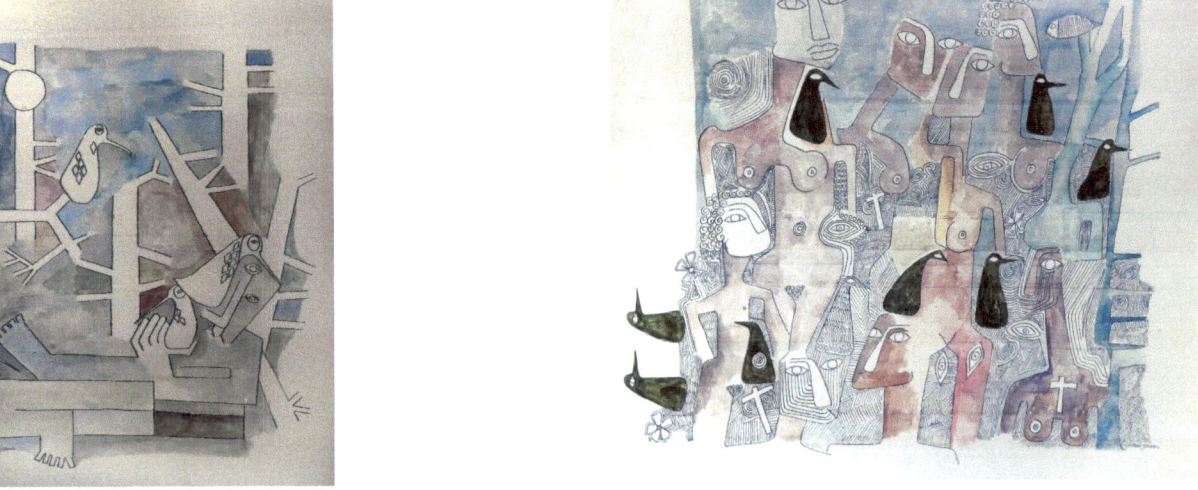
RS174

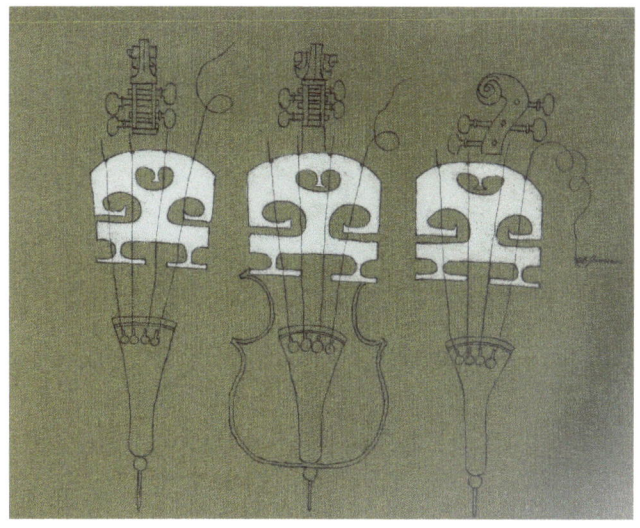

RS175

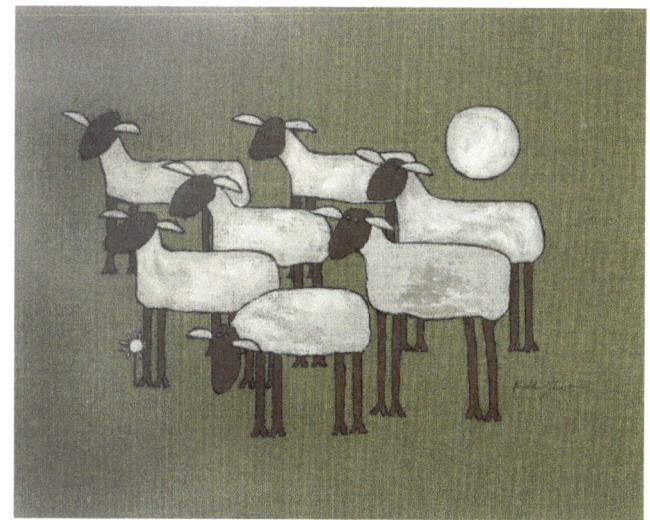

RS176

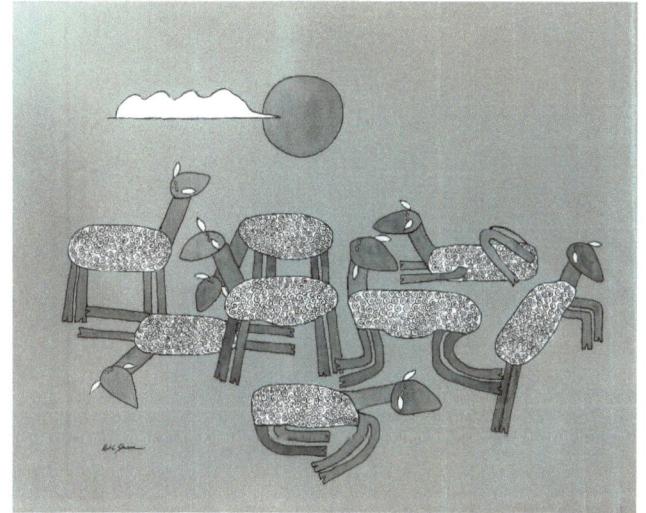

RS177

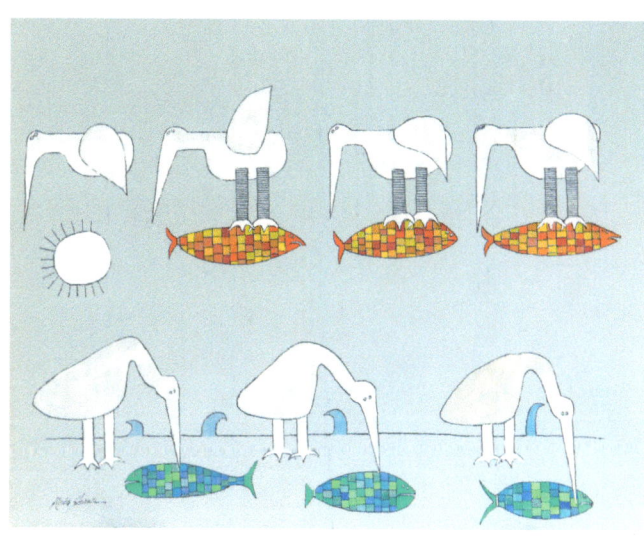

RS178

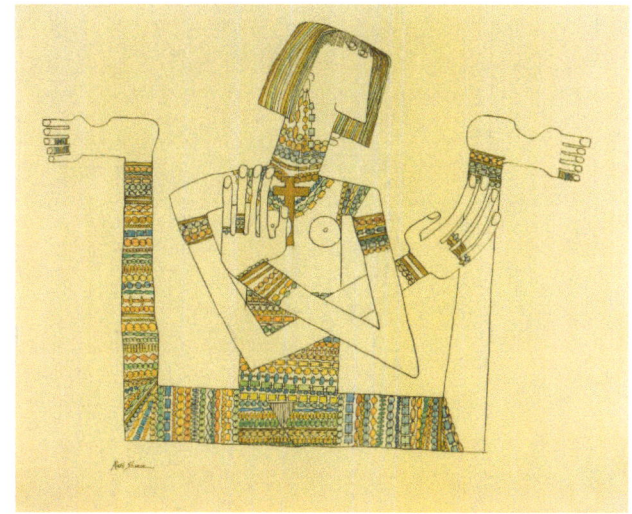

RS179

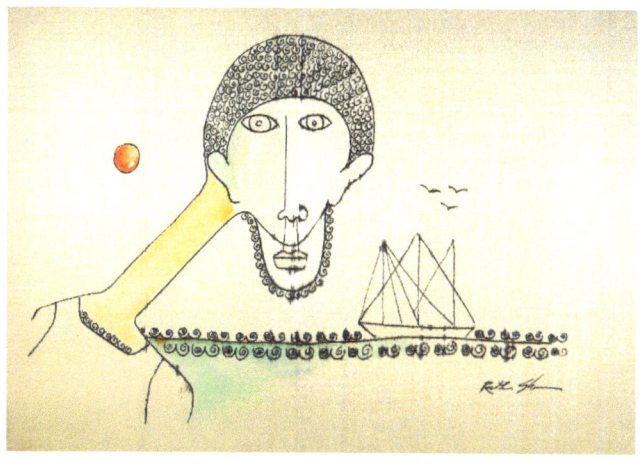

RS180

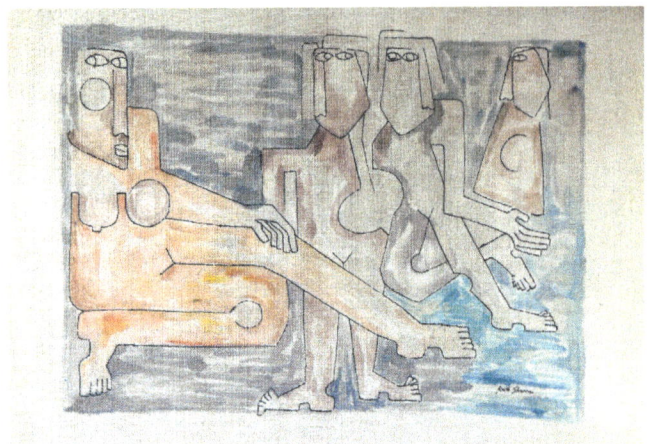

RS181

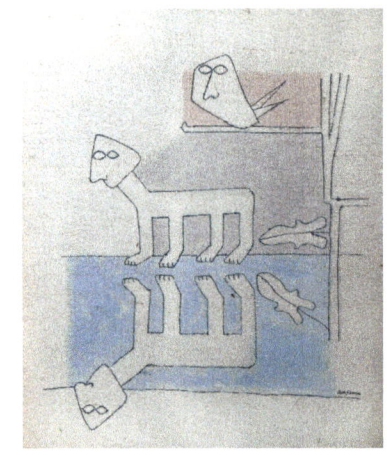

RS182

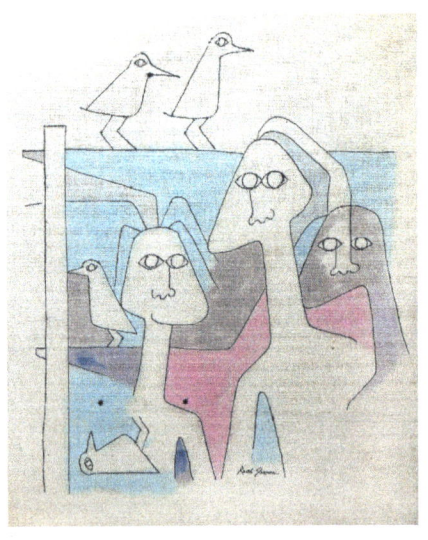

RS183

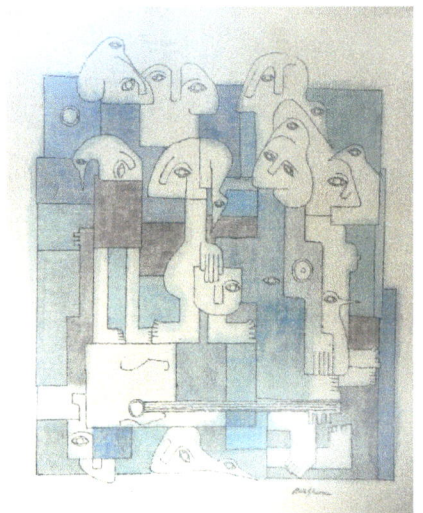

RS184

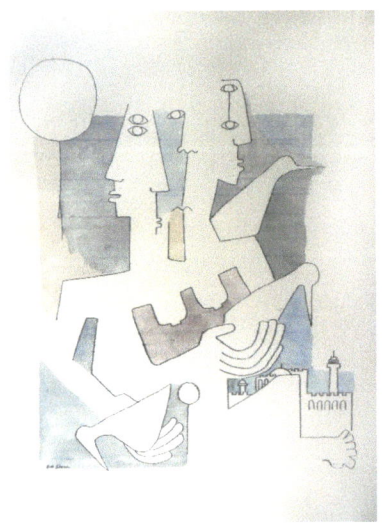

RS185

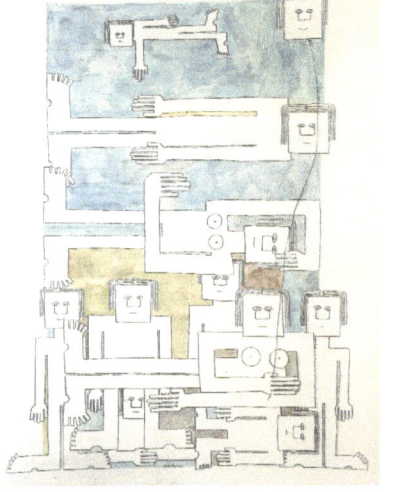

RS186

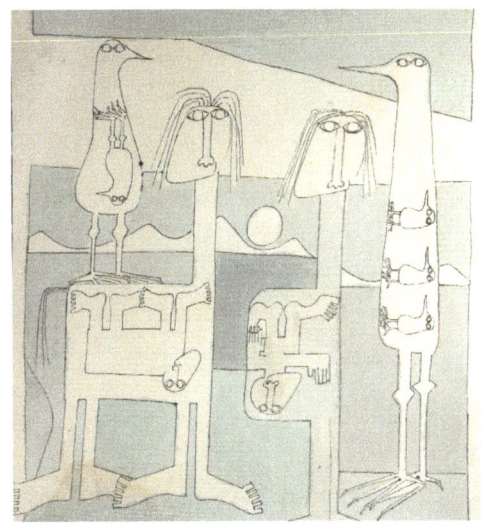

RS187

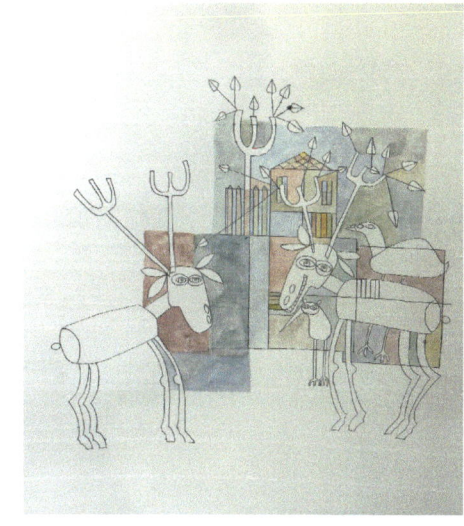

RS188

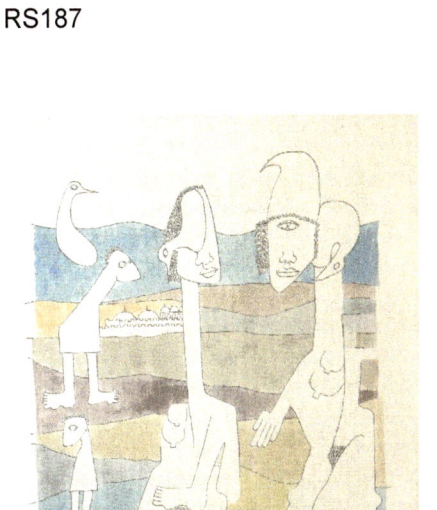

RS189

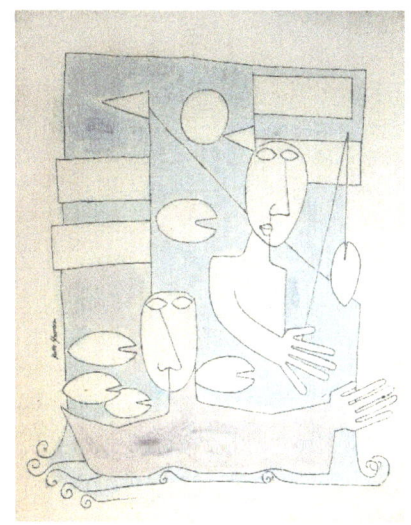

RS190

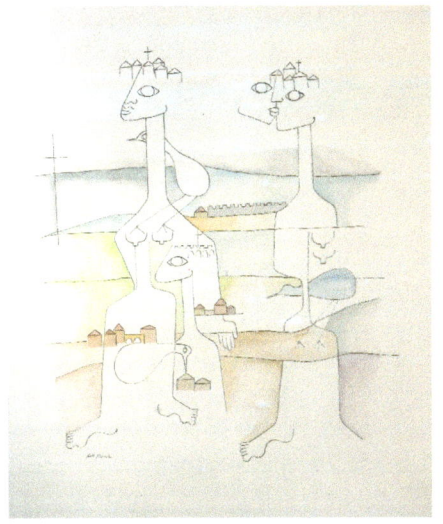

RS191

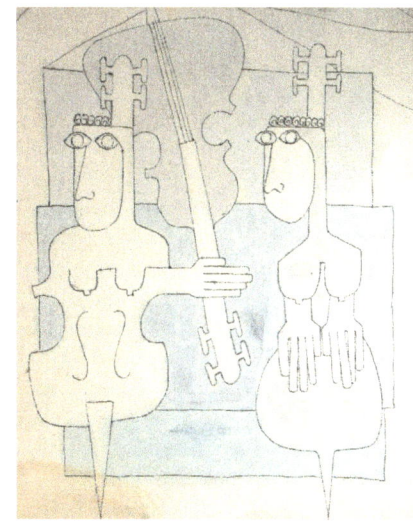

RS192

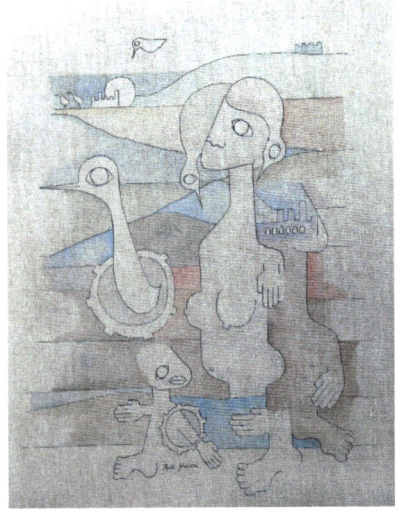

RS193

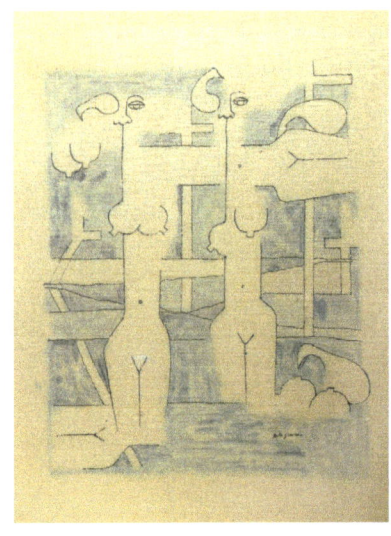

RS194

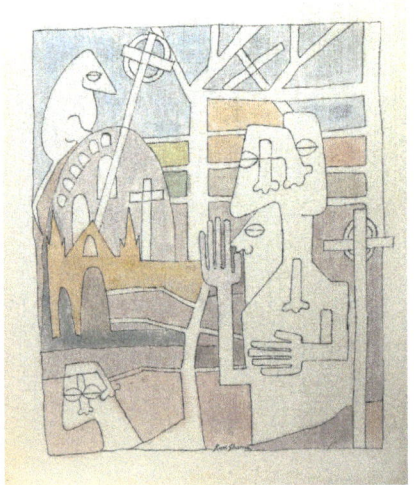

RS195

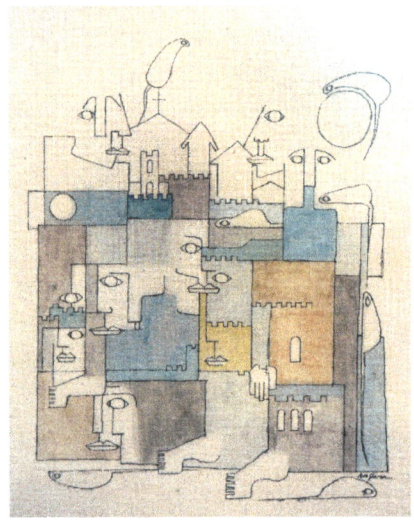

RS196

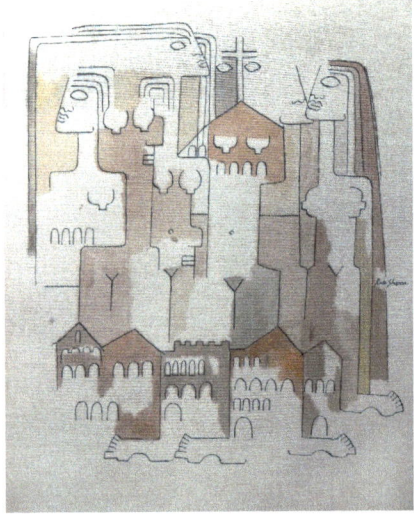

RS197

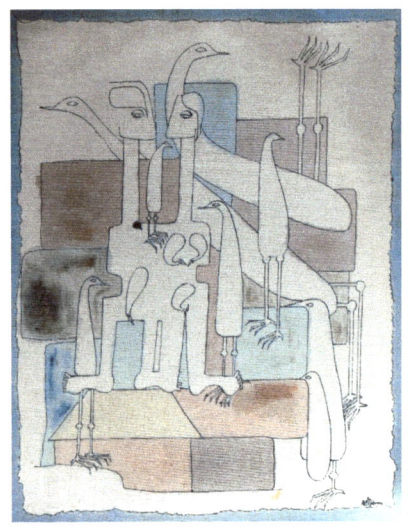

RS198

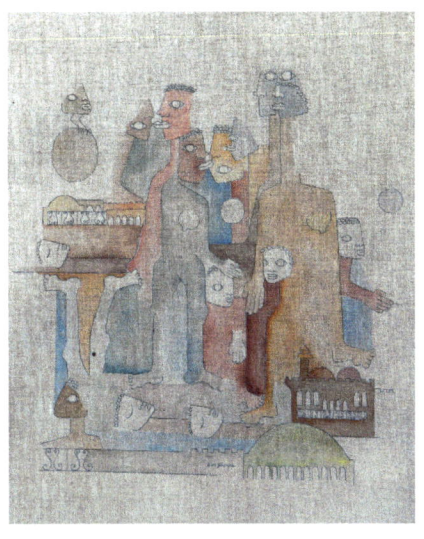

RS199

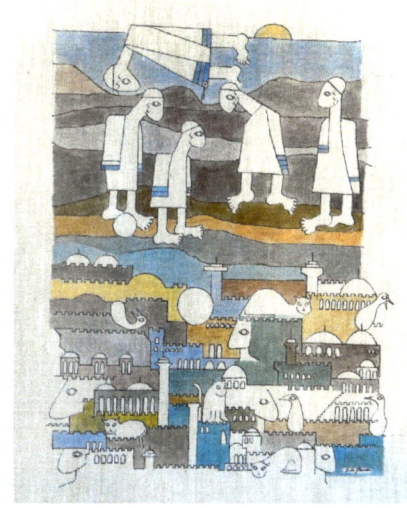

RS200

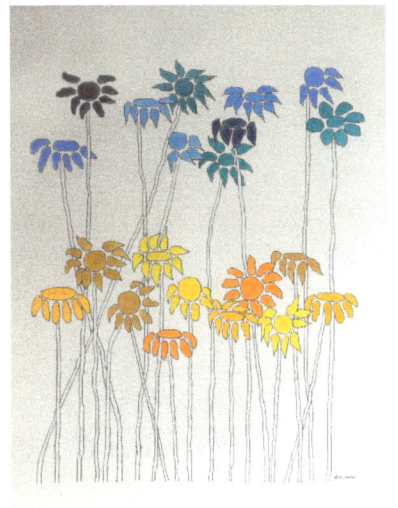

RS201

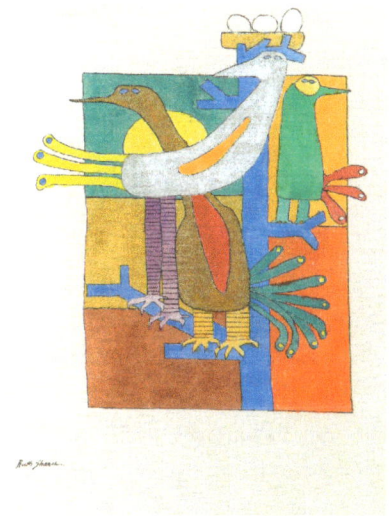

RS202

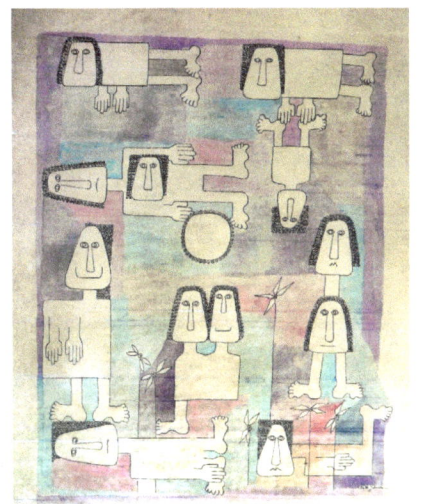

RS203

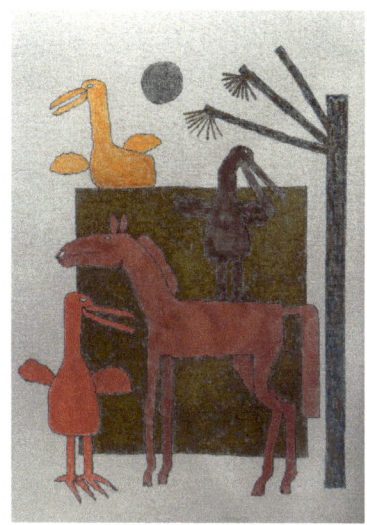

RS204

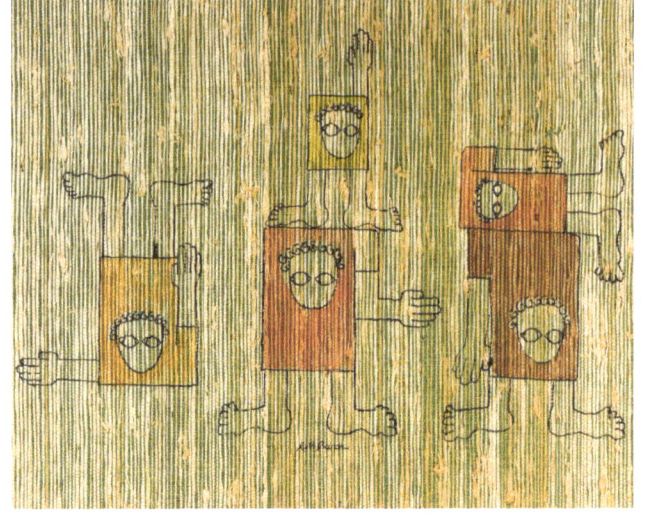

RS205

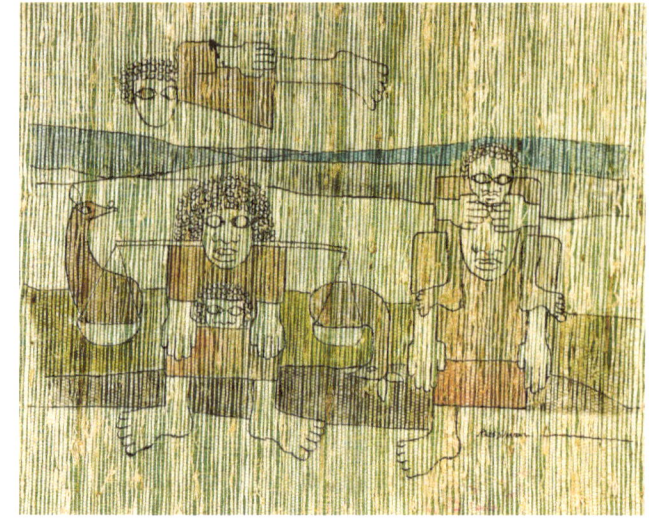

RS206

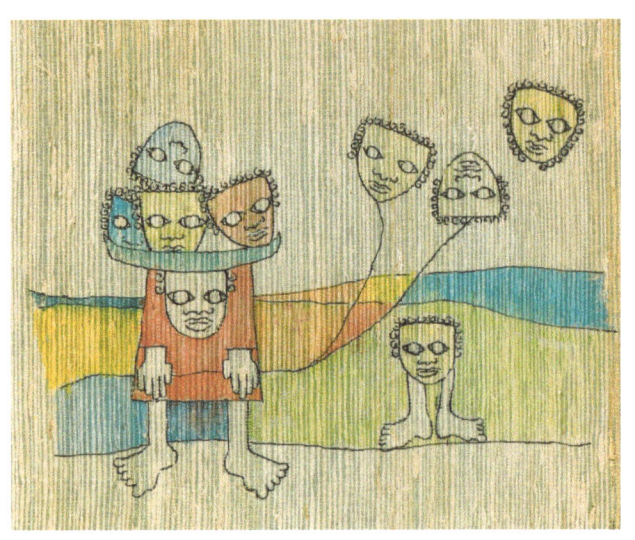

RS207

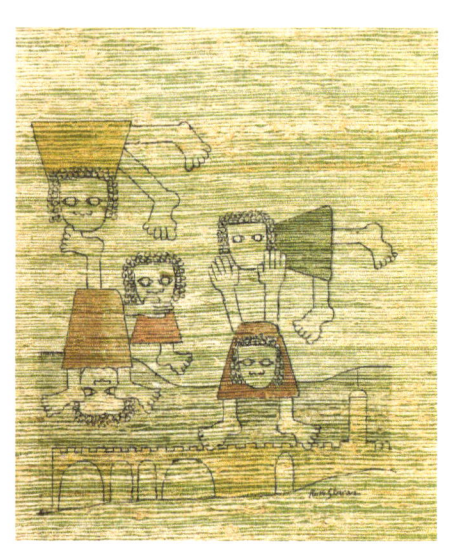

RS208

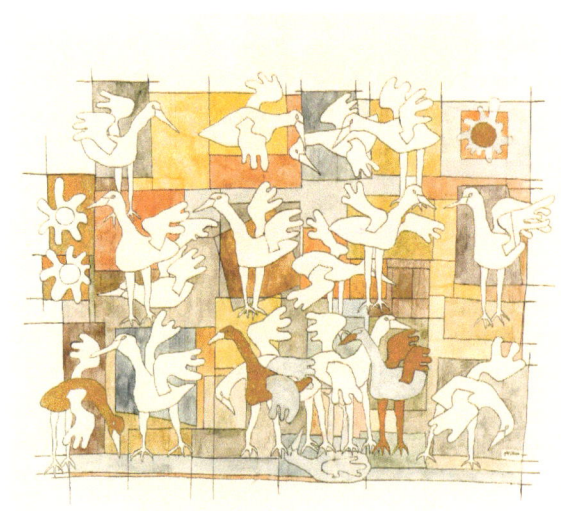

RS209

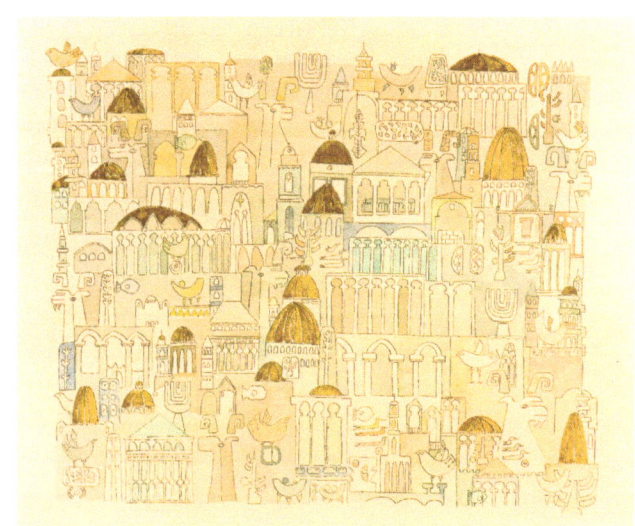

RS210

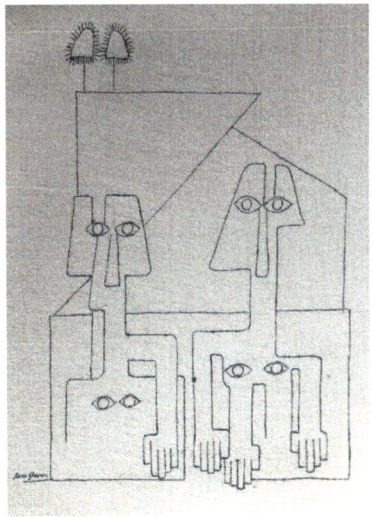

RS211

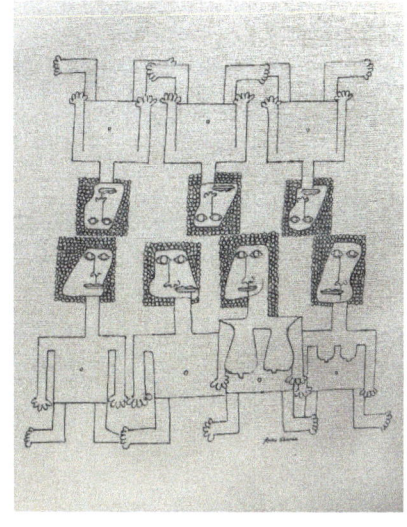

RS212

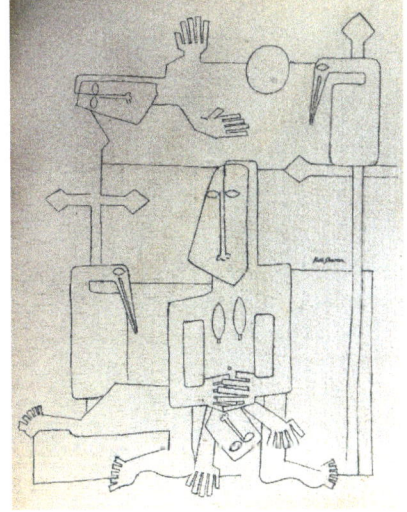

RS213

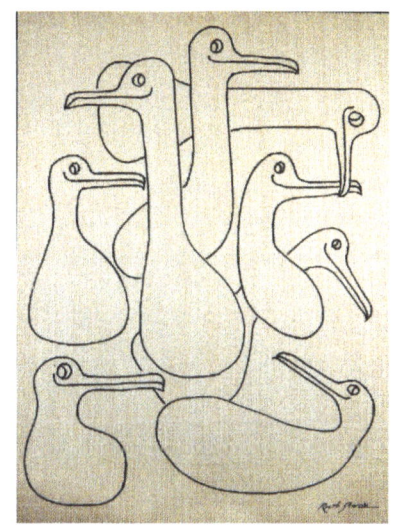

RS214

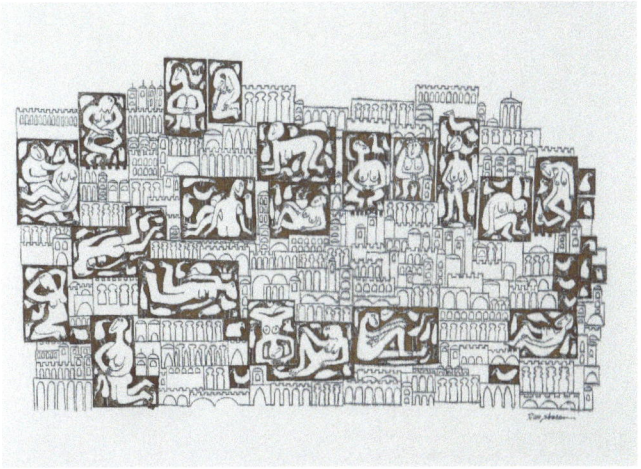

RS215

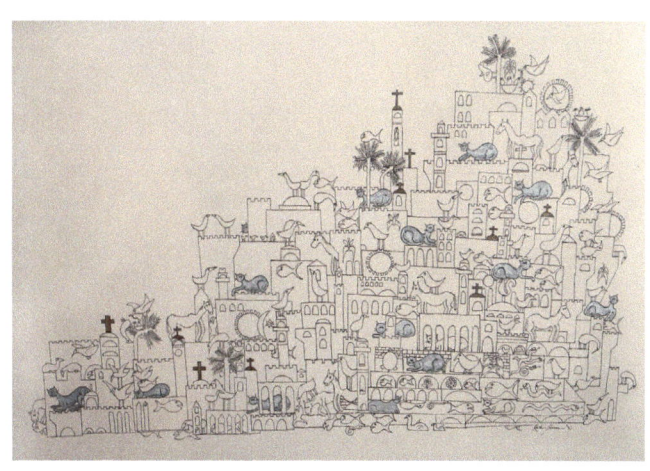

RS216

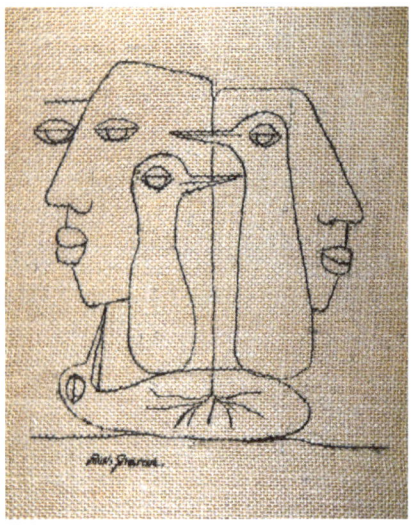

RS217

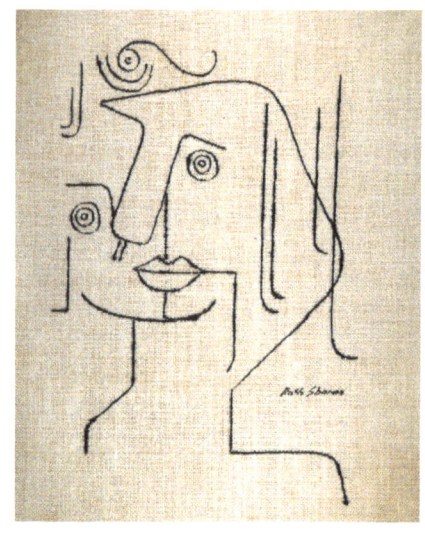

RS218

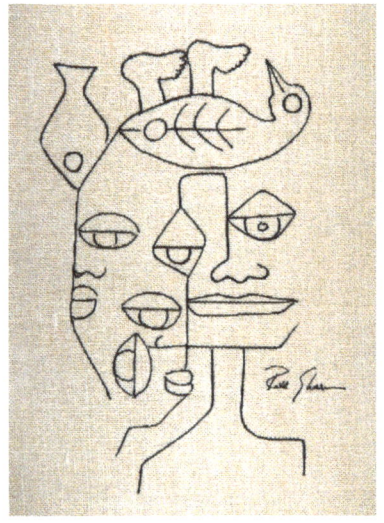

RS219

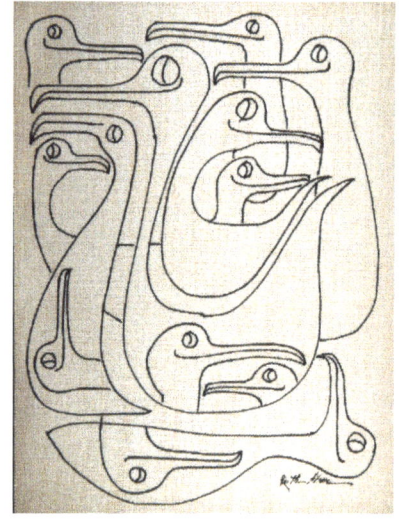

RS220

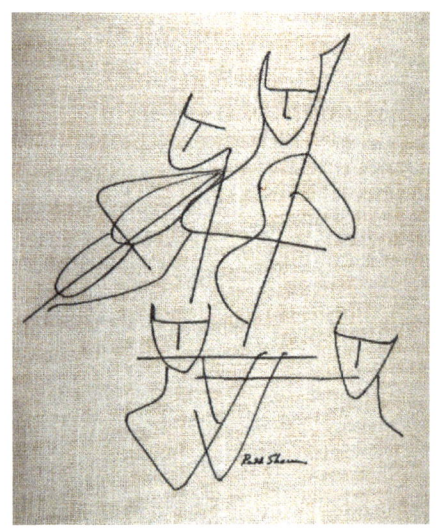

RS221

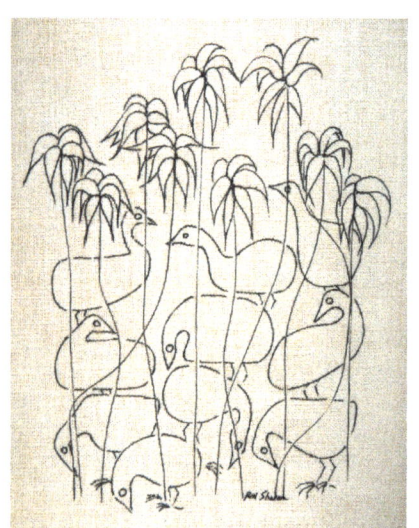

RS222

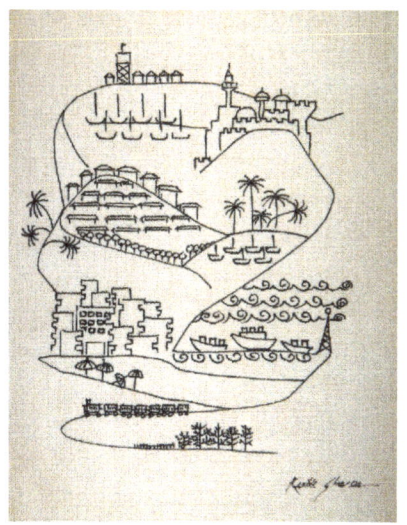

RS223

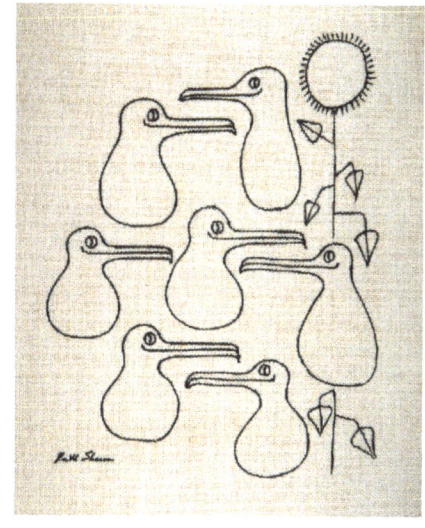

RS224

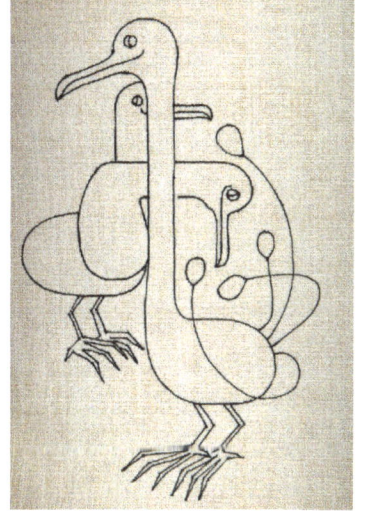

RS225

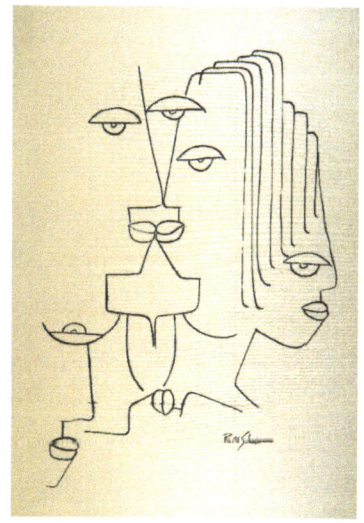

RS226

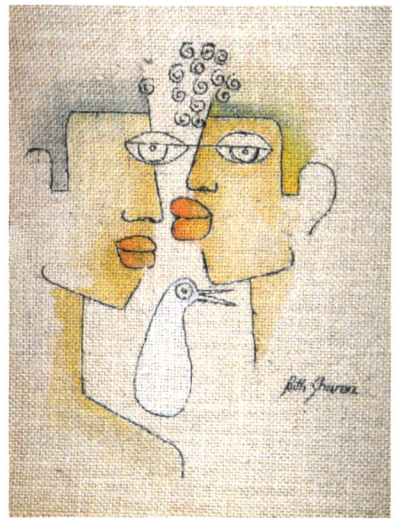

RS227

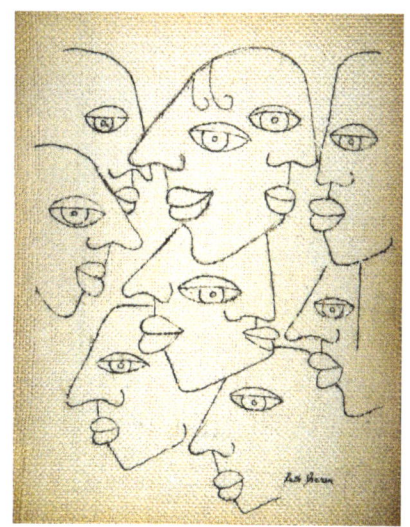

RS228

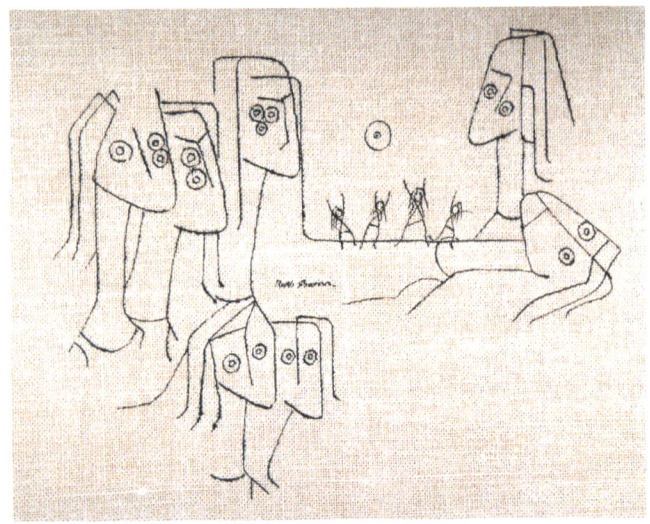

RS229

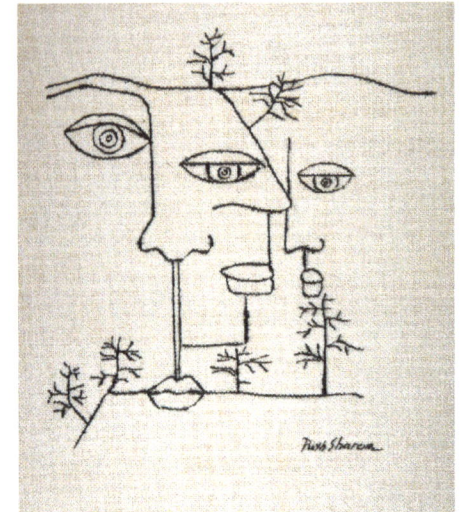

RS230

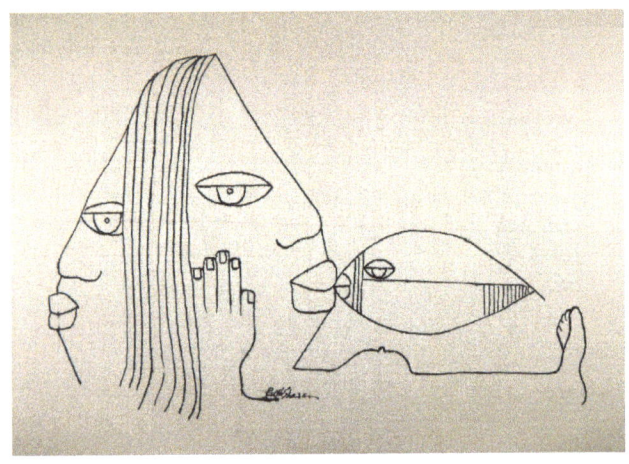

RS231

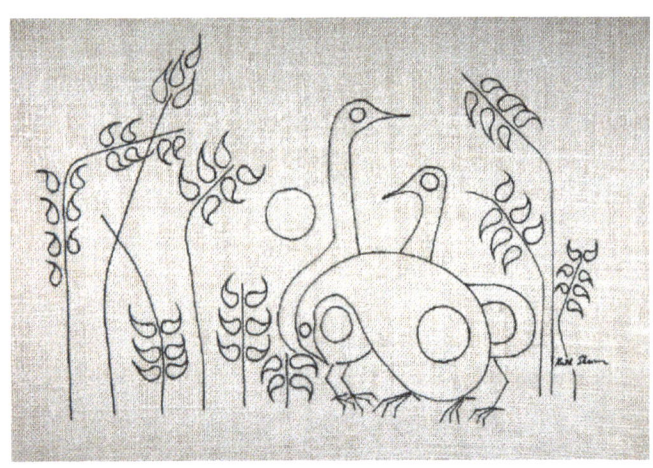

RS232

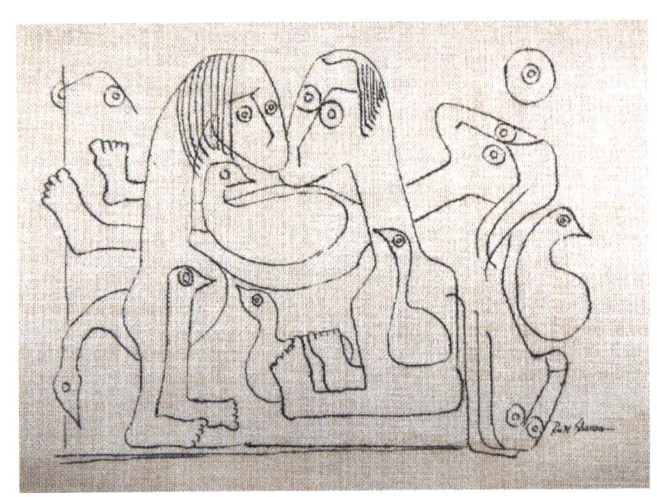

RS233

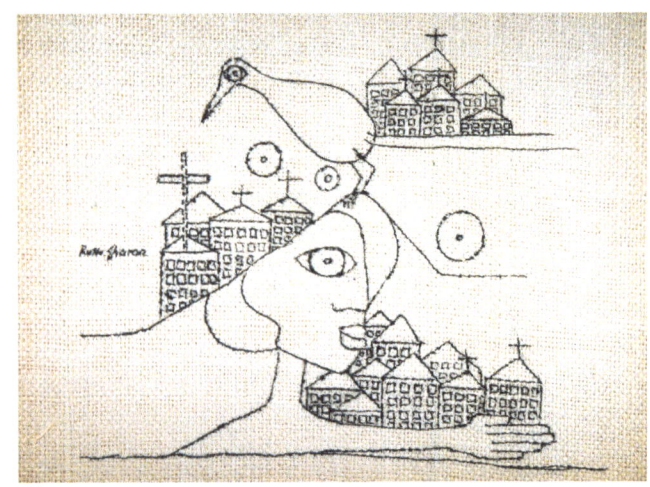

RS234

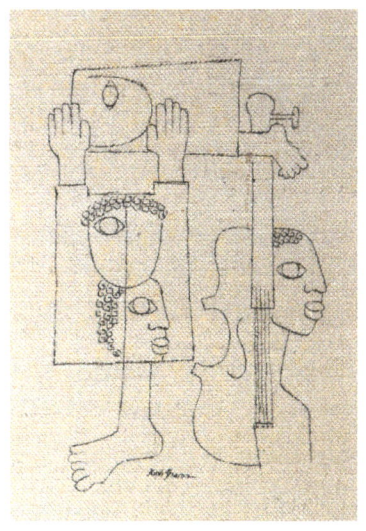

RS235

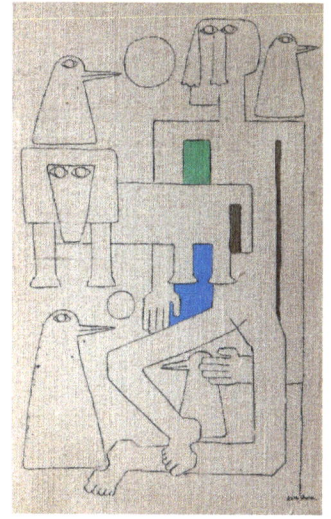

RS236

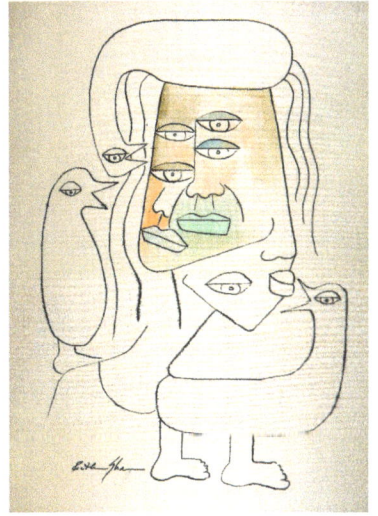

RS237

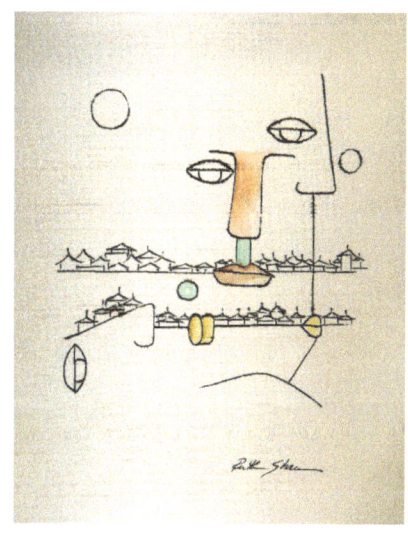

RS238

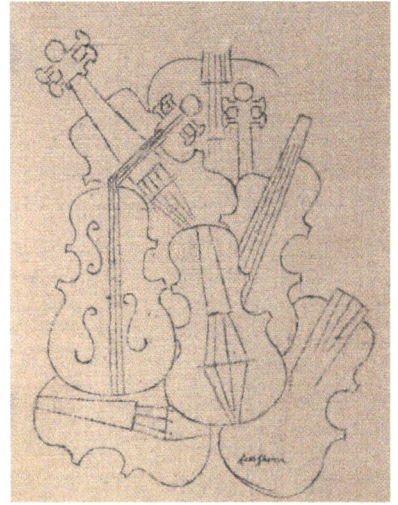

RS239

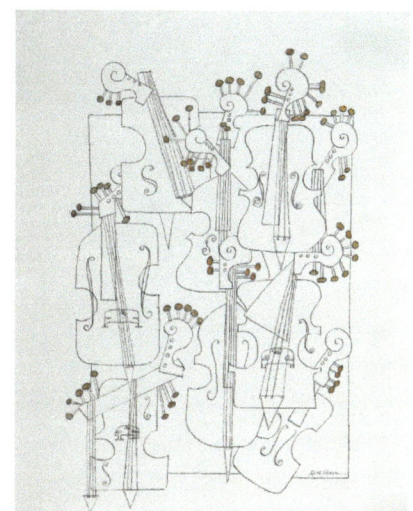

RS240

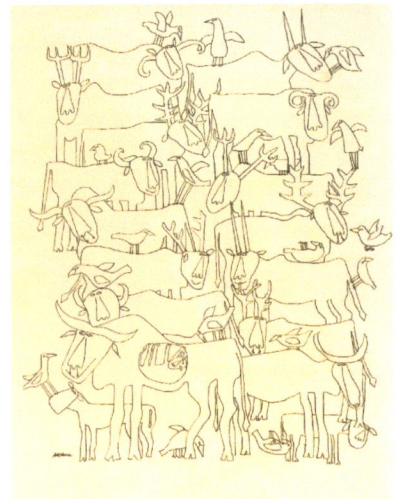

RS241

RS242

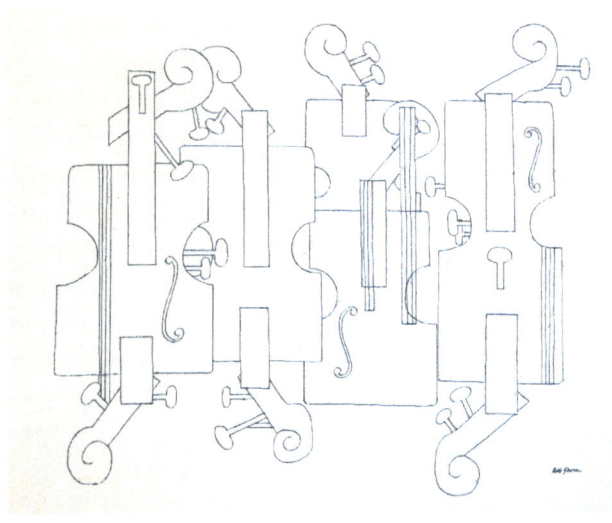

RS243

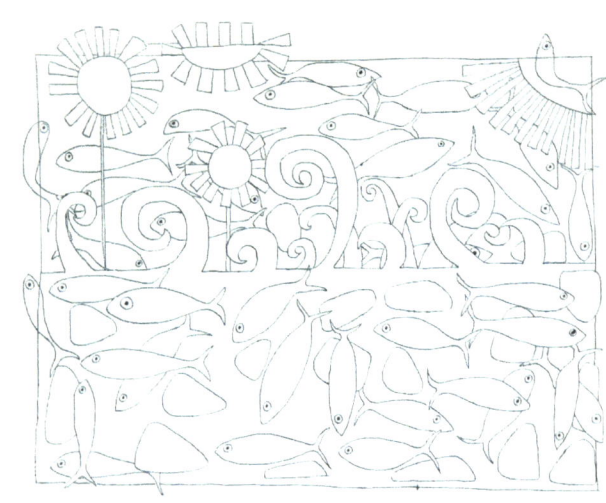

RS244

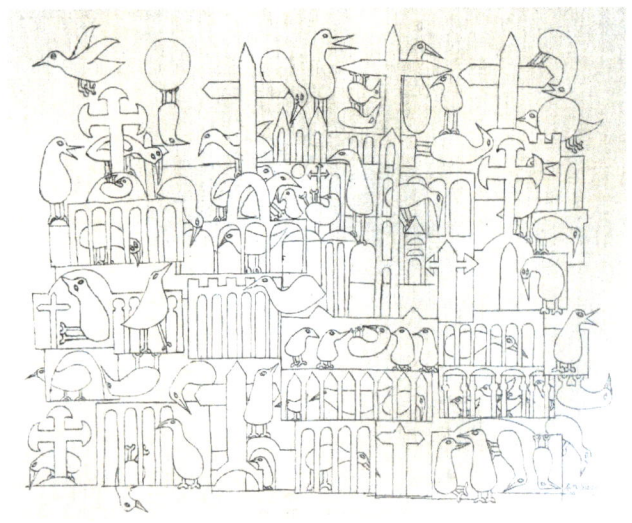

RS245

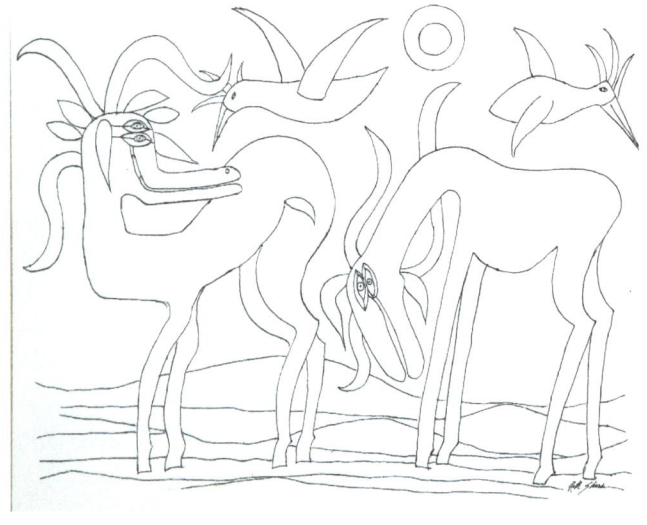

RS246

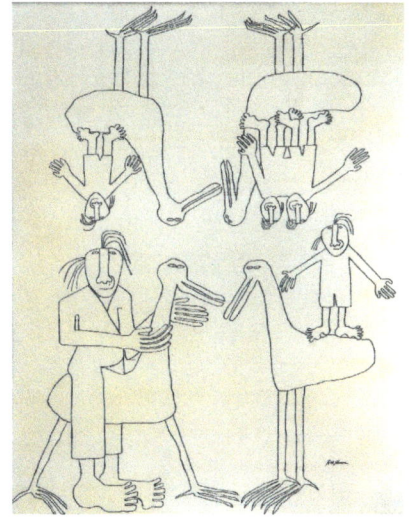

RS247

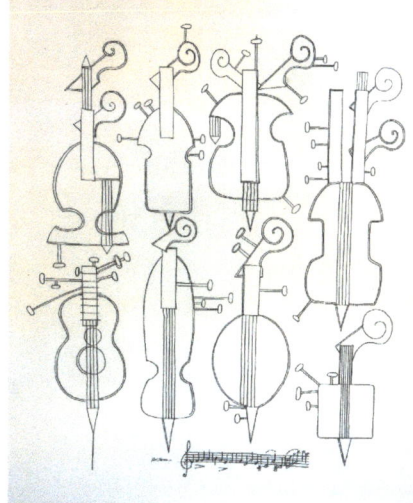

RS248

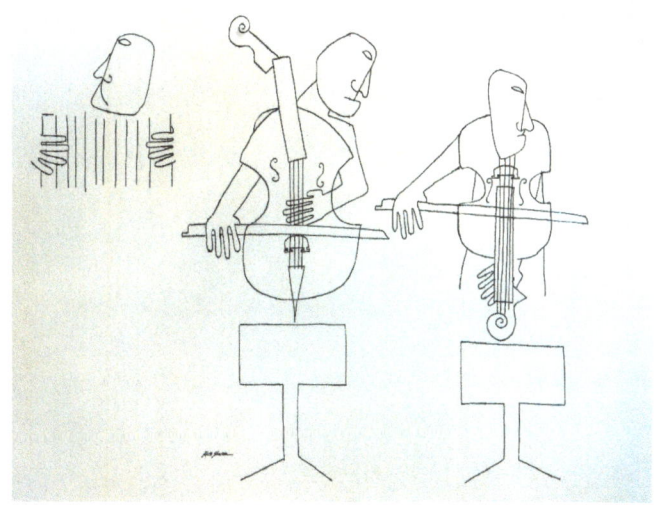

RS249

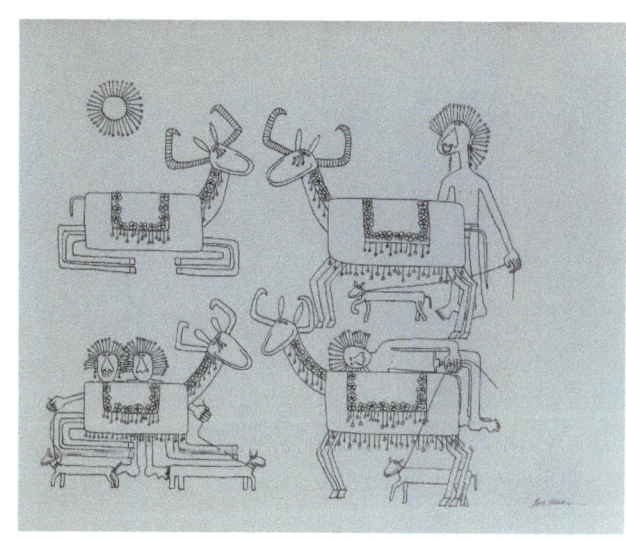

RS250

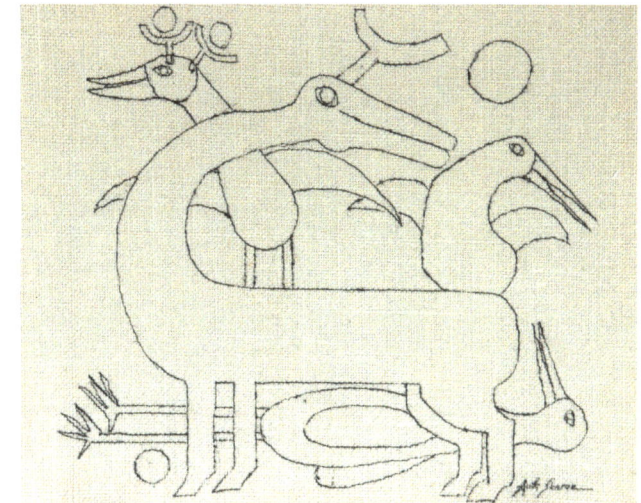

RS251

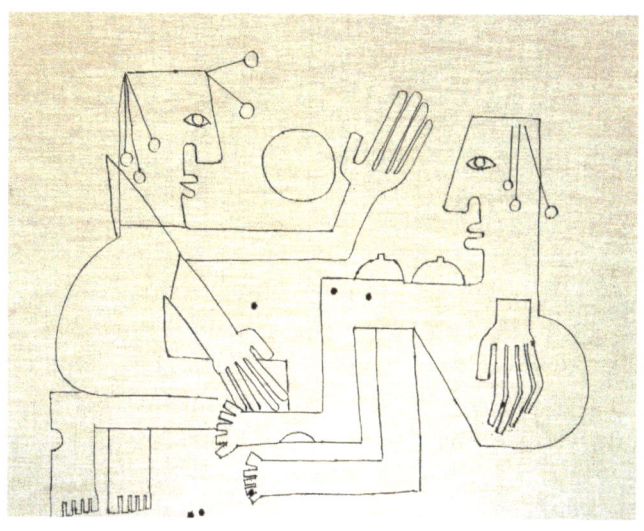

RS252

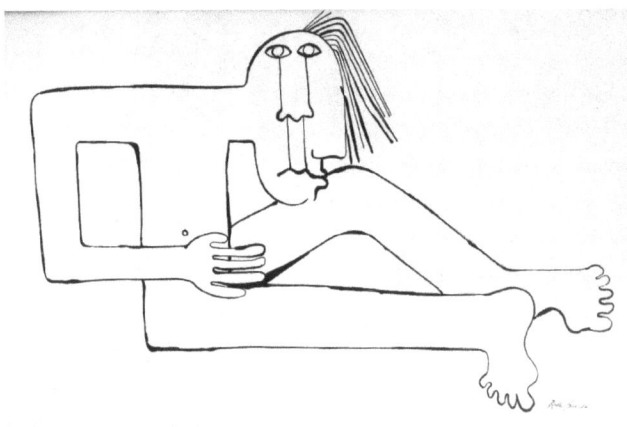

RS253

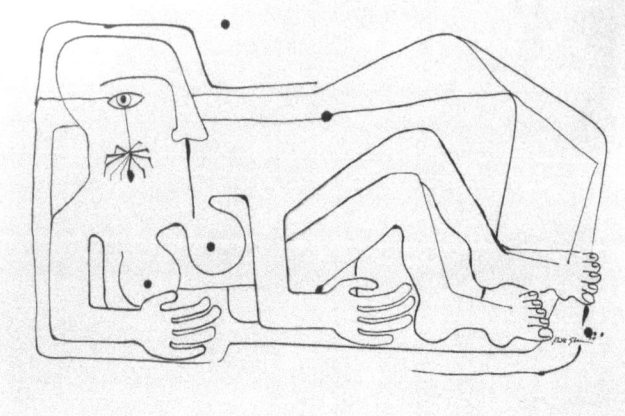

RS254

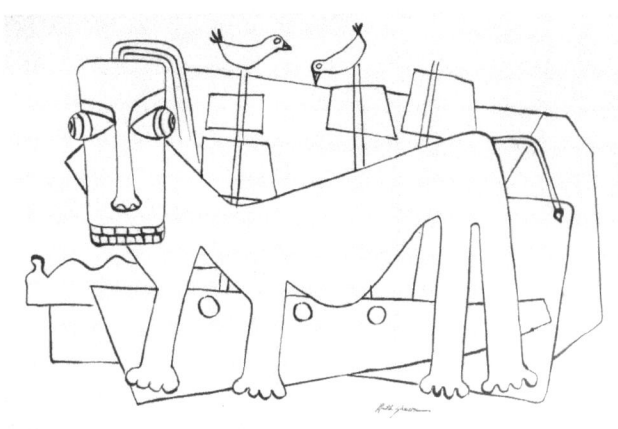

RS255

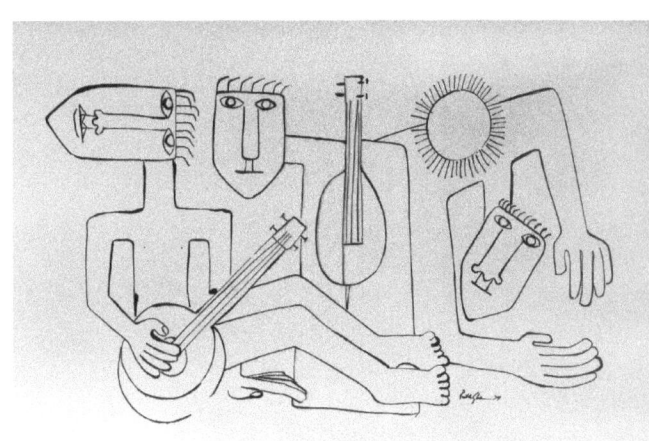

RS256

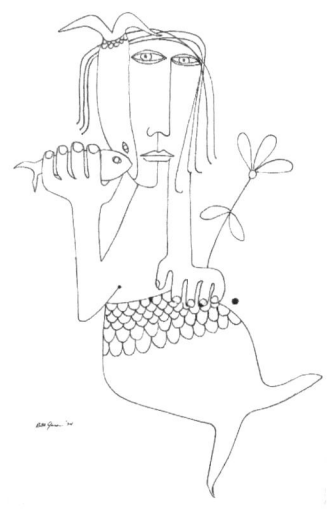

RS257

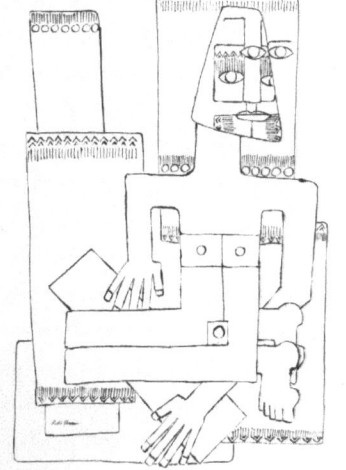

RS258

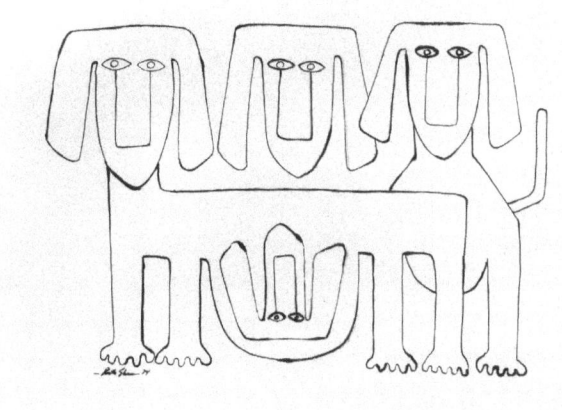
RS259

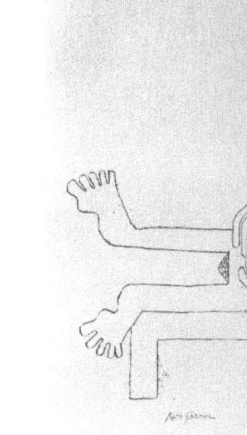
RS260

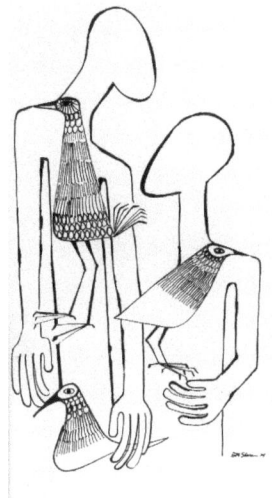
RS261

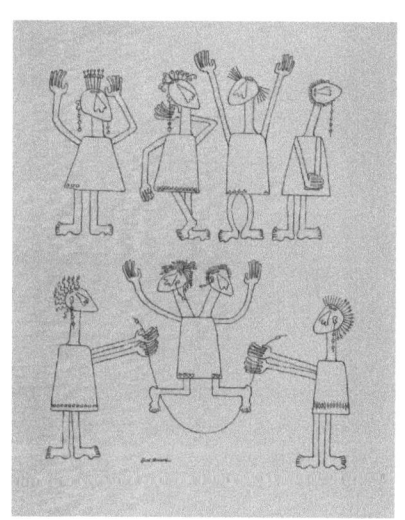
RS262

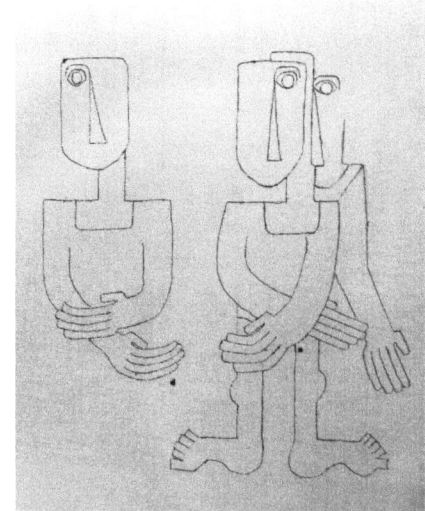
RS263

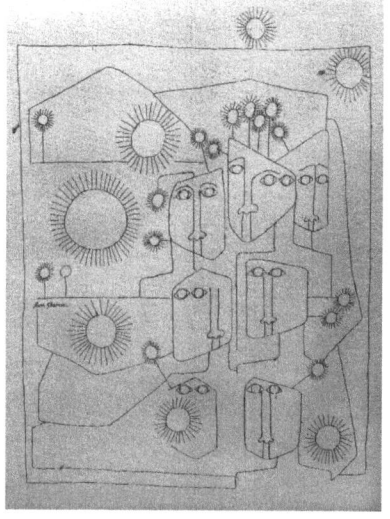
RS264

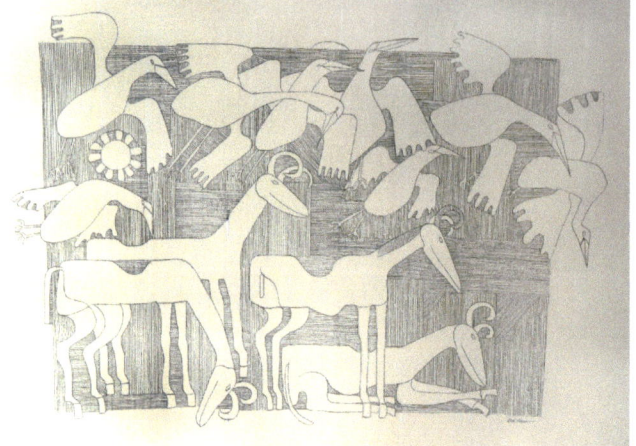

RS265

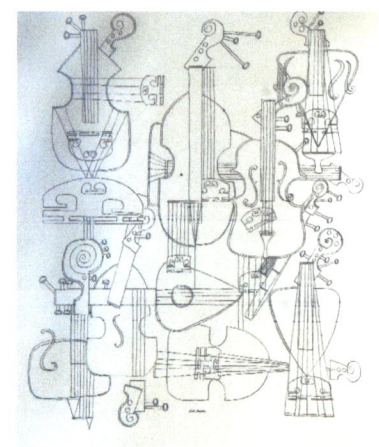

RS266

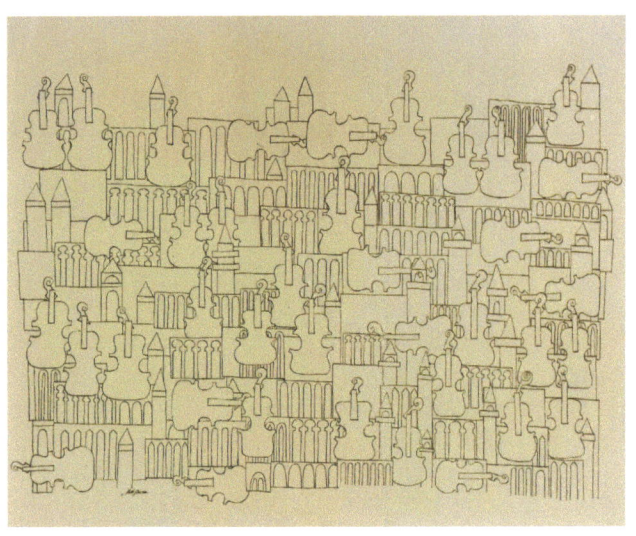

RS267

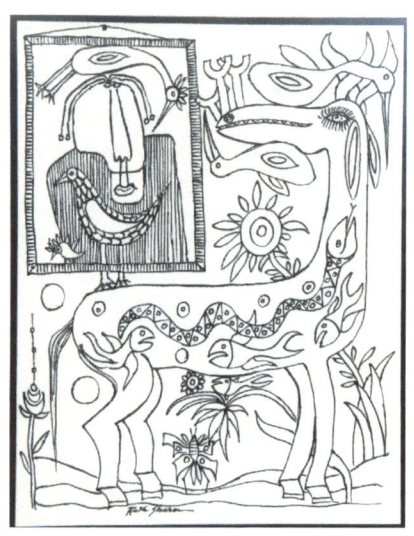

RS268

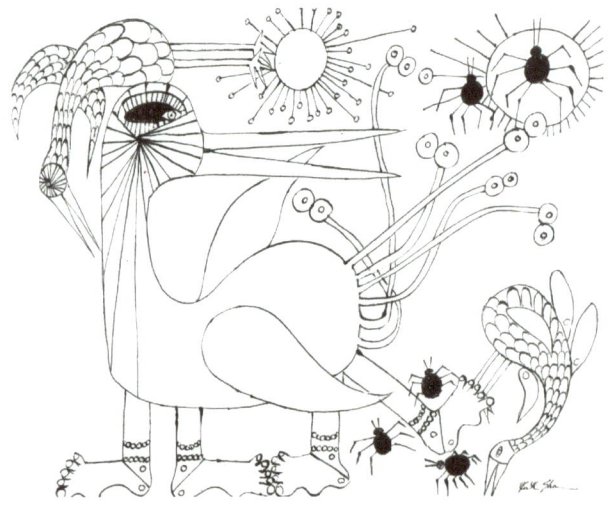

RS269

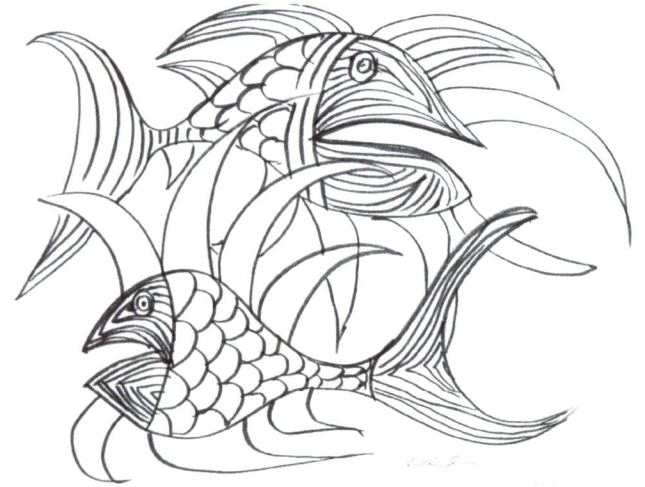

RS270

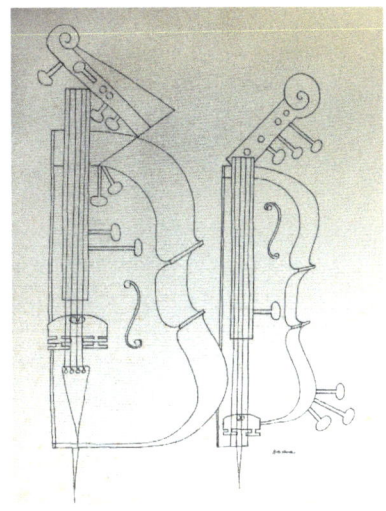

RS271

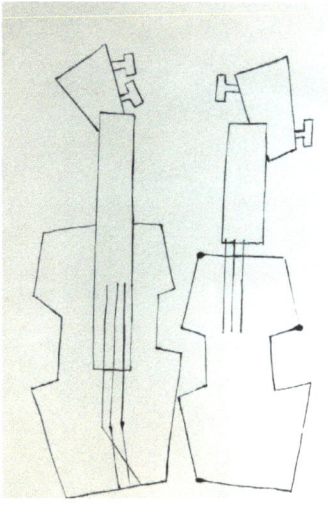

RS272

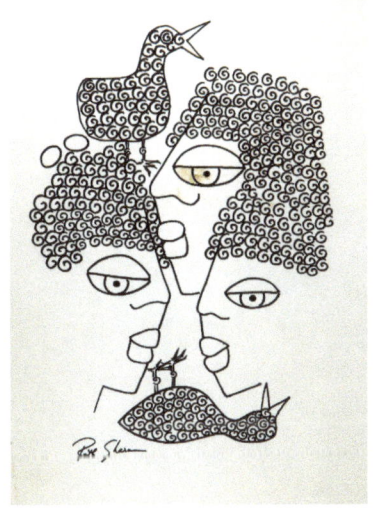

RS273

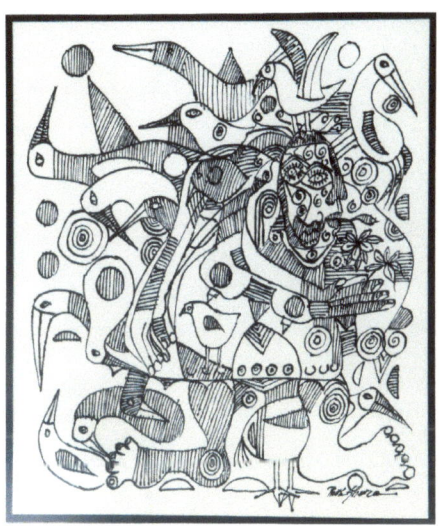

RS274

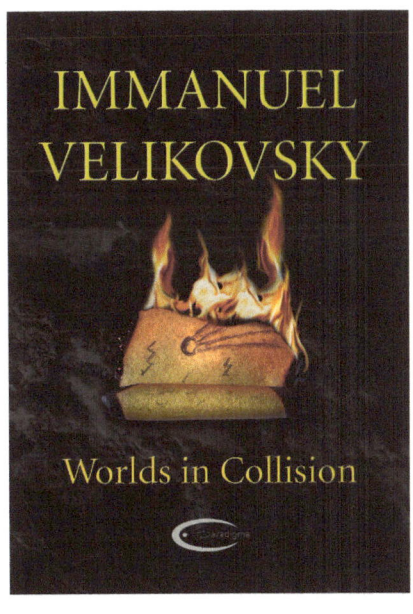

Worlds in Collision

by Immanuel Velikovsky

ISBN 978-1-906833-11-4

With this book Immanuel Velikovsky first presented the revolutionary results of his 10-year-long interdisciplinary research to the public - and caused an uproar that is still going on today.

Worlds in Collision - written in a brilliant, easily understandable and entertaining style and full to the brim with precise information - can be considered one of the most important and most challenging books in the history of science. Not without reason was this book found open on Einstein's desk after his death.

For all those who have ever wondered about the evolution of the earth, the history of mankind, traditions, religions, mythology or just the world as it is today, *Worlds in Collision* is an absolute MUST-READ!

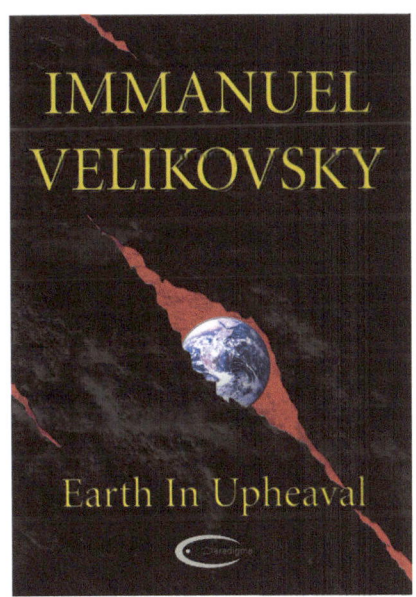

Earth in Upheaval

by Immanuel Velikovsky

ISBN 978-1-906833-12-1

After the publication of *Worlds in Collision* Immanuel Velikovsky was confronted with the argument that in the shape of the earth and in the flora and fauna there are no traces of the natural catastrophes he had described.

Therefore a few years later he published *Earth in Upheaval* which not only supports the historical documents by very impressive geological and paleontological material, but even arrives at the same conclusions just based on the testimony of stones and bones.

Earth in Upheaval - a very exactly investigated and easily understandable book - contains material that completely revolutionizes our view of the history of the earth.

For all those who have ever wondered about the evolution of the earth, the formation of mountains and oceans, the origin of coal or fossils, the question of the ice ages and the history of animal and plant species, Earth in Upheaval is a MUST-READ!

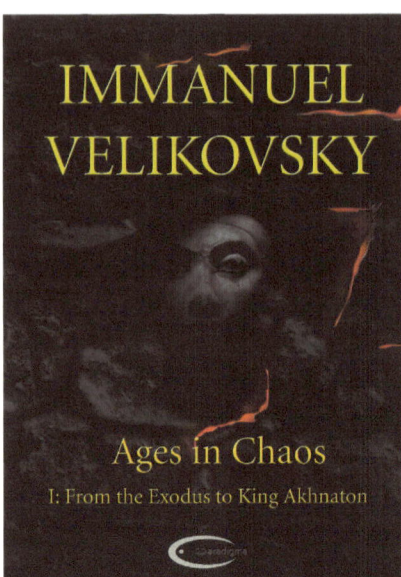

Ages in Chaos

by Immanuel Velikovsky

ISBN 978-1-906833-13-8

This is the first volume of the series *Ages in Chaos*, in which Immanuel Velikovsky undertakes a reconstruction of the history of antiquity.
With utmost precision and the exciting style of a presentation that's typical for him he shows, beyond doubt, what nobody would consider possible: In the conventional history of Egypt - and therefore also of many neighboring cultures - a span of 600 years is described, which has never happened! This assertion is as unbelievable and outrageous as the assertions in *Worlds in Collision* or *Earth in Upheaval*. But Velikovsky takes us on a detailed and highly interesting journey through the - corrected - history and makes us a witness to how many question marks disappear, doubts vanish and corresponding facts from the entire Near East furnish a picture of overall conformity and correctness. In the end you do not only wonder how conventional historiography has come into existence, but why it is still taught and published.
Just as Velikovsky became the father of "neo-catastrophism" by *Worlds in Collision*, he became the father of "new chronology" by *Ages in Chaos*.

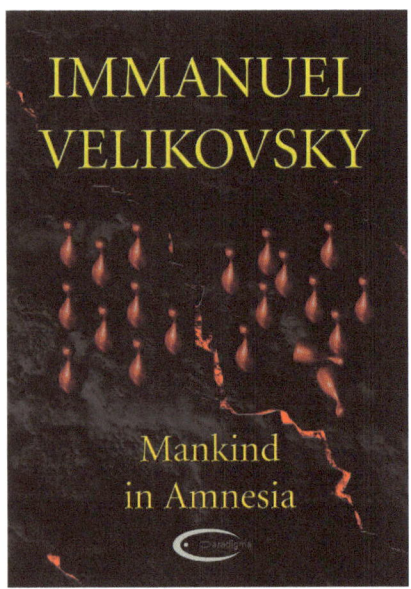

Mankind in Amnesia

by Immanuel Velikovsky

ISBN 978-1-906833-16-9

Immanuel Velikovsky called this book the "fulfillment of his oath of Hippocrates - to serve humanity." In this book he returns to his roots as a psychologist and psychoanalytical therapist, yet not with a single person as his patient but with humanity as a whole. After an extremely revealing overview of the foundations of the various psychoanalytical systems he takes the step into crowd psychology and reopens the case of *Worlds in Collision* from a totally different point of view: a psychoanalytical case study. This way he shows that the blatant reactions to his theories (which are still going on today) have not been surprising but actually inevitable from a psychological perspective - which equally holds for those who have defined our view of the world. At the same time he is able to reclassify the theories of Siegmund Freud and C. G. Jung by finding a common basis for them.
A journey through history, religion, mythology and art shows the overall range of the collective trauma and is giving us - the patients - a message of extraordinary urgency and importance for the future.

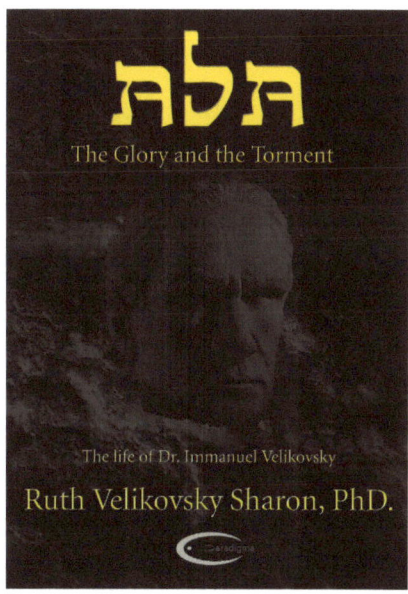

ABA - The Glory and the Torment

by Ruth Velikovsky Sharon, PhD

ISBN 978-1-906833-20-6

In this book you get to know Immanuel Velikovsky as a person. His daughter Ruth describes his childhood, his family environment and his eventful life.

Using plenty of background information, numerous anecdotes and many photographs she makes us familiar with her father, but also shows the personal dimension of the devastating campaign he encountered to in the last decades of his life.

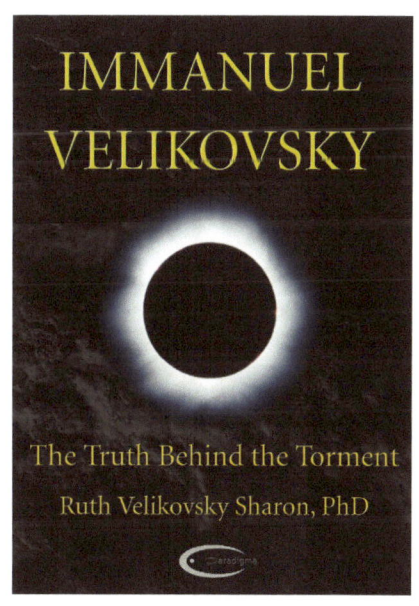

The Truth Behind the Torment

by Ruth Velikovsky Sharon, PhD

ISBN 978-1-906833-21-3

In this supplement to her father's biography, Ruth Velikovsky Sharon, PhD. depicts the true facts about the campaign against him.

She publishes revealing letters in full length, that show the true nature of the undeserving - unscientific - treatment of Velikovsky by the scientific establishment, a treatment that appears rather medieval than enlightened.

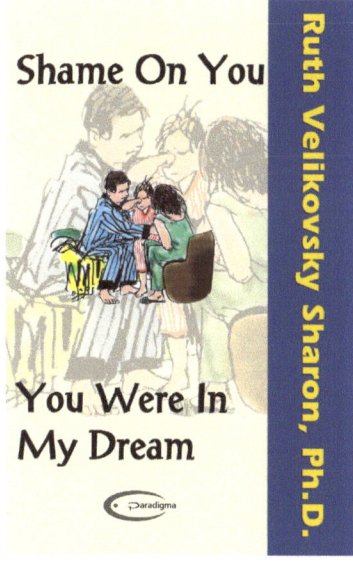

Shame on You - You Were in My Dream

by Ruth Velikovsky Sharon, PhD

ISBN 978-1-906833-01-5

Finally a new and easy guide to the understanding of dreams, which really makes sense!
Ruth Velikovsky Sharon, PhD has developed a completely new understanding of the nature of dreams, which is fascinating because of its simplicity and its practical orientation.

She questions ideas we have long taken for granted. She asks us to reconsider what the word "dream" really means. She shows us that to use the word "dream" in partnership with "He is a dreamboat" or "My dream house!" is to misuse or even abuse the word "dream".

In her book, Dr. Sharon describes the way that parents can be of help vis a vis dreams: Listen and Learn. Ask your children how they felt in the dream, ask them what they thought in the dream.

She includes chapters on manipulation in dreams, dream catchers and other gadgets and the environment and dreams.

Also included is a reprint of the article "A New Understanding of Dreams", published by Dr. Sharon in *New Jersey Medicine*, Journal of the Medical Society of New Jersey, January 1995 issue.

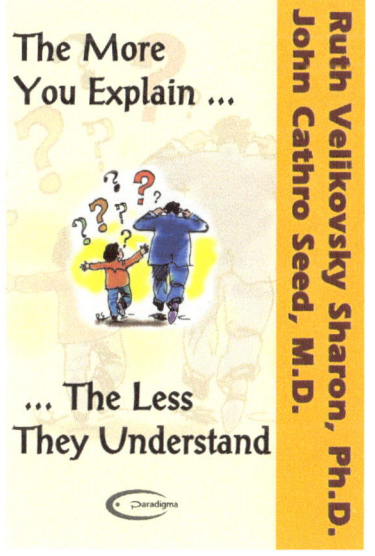

The More You Explain - The Less They Understand

by Ruth Velikovsky Sharon, PhD and John Cathro Seed, MD

ISBN 978-1-906833-00-8

In this, perhaps the most encompassing of her works, Dr. Ruth Velikovsky Sharon brilliantly lifts the veil that shrouds the mystery of psychoanalysis, revealing intrinsic truths that can forever assist us in our journey to self-discovery and growth.

Like a finely tuned and well-trained instrument, Dr. Sharon makes her probe into the human psyche sound easy - resulting in a compilation of luminous insights that are warm in their humanity, vibrant in their simplicity, and even touched with humor.

Harvard Medical School trained, Dr. John C. Seed's contribution of the Physical Health chapter will enlighten the medical community as well as the average reader, and if abided by, will help prolong life.

www.ingramcontent.com/pod-product-compliance
Lightning Source LLC
Chambersburg PA
CBHW051201220526
45473CB00003B/852